BUMOSAUR IS THAT?

Andy Griffiths became aware of the urgent need for
a comprehensive guide to bumosaurs during the writing
of the final volume of his internationally bestselling
BUM trilogy. The magnificent work of non-fiction that
you now hold in your hands is the result of at least half
an hour of painstaking research. It draws together all the
known information – both factual and non-factual – on
this unfortunate period in the history of life on Earth.
Andy was delighted when Dr Terence Denton agreed to
travel back in time with him to help to bring these
arsetounding creatures to life.

Terry Denton is a well-known and very serious scientific
illarsetrator. It was the highlight of his career to be
invited along as the official artist on this First Great
Bumosaur Expedition by Dr Andrew Griffiths. While he
has vast experience illarsetrating scientific texts such as
the JUST! books, nothing could quite prepare him for
the exhilaration of coming face to face with creatures
such as the Tricerabutt and the Tyrannosore-arse rex with
only a pen and paper to defend himself. After a
particularly frightening incident with the Great woolly
butthead (not Andy!) he was badly wounded and is
presently recovering in hospital.

WHAT BUMOSAUR IS THAT?

ANDY GRIFFITHS & TERRY DENTON

MACMILLAN CHILDREN'S BOOKS

First published 2007 by Pan Macmillan Australia Pty Limited

This edition published in the UK 2007 by Macmillan Children's Books
a division of Macmillan Publishers Limited
20 New Wharf Road, London NI 9RR
Basingstoke and Oxford
www.panmacmillan.com

Associated companies throughout the world

ISBN: 978-0-330-44752-2

Text copyright © Backyard Stories Pty Ltd 2007
Illustrations copyright © Terry Denton 2007

1 3 5 7 9 8 6 4 2

A CIP catalogue record for this book is available from
the British Library.

Printed and bound in Great Britain by Mackays of Chatham plc, Kent

Contents

Tyrannosore-arse rex versus Tricerabutt 114

Bumornithids 117

Exstinktion of the bumosaurs 132

Bummals 135

Famarse bumosaurologists 148

Index 151

Introduction

Life on Earth began with primitive bumteria that appeared in the oceans during the Pre-Crappian time, 600 million years ago. Over time, these bumteria bumvolved into more complex forms of bum life, including invertebutts, bumfish, bumphibians, stenchtiles, farthropods and stinksects, until eventually giving rise to the group of stenchtiles we know as the bumosaurs and bumornithids.

Bumosaurs appeared on the Earth 250 million years ago at the beginning of the Triarssic period. They came in a stunning variety of shapes and sizes, with an equally stunning variety of stinks and stenches.

Dominating bum life on Earth for the next 185 million years, bumosaurs disappeared from the fossil record around 65 million years ago. (Though it has been speculated that some very exceptional exceptions survived.) The exstinktion of the bumosaurs allowed a new species of bum life called bummals to bumvolve, eventually leading to the emergence of the earliest bum-men.

Although the focus of this book is on bumosaurs, examples of bum-related life forms from all major groups have been included in order to provide the most comprehensive – and up-to-date – guide to prehistoric bum life ever published.

pibum Spiny bum-urchin Octostenchosaurus Bum
in Octostenchosaurus Bum-sponge Trilobut
ostenchosaurus Bum-sponge Trilobutt Jelly bumf
-sponge Trilobutt Jelly bumfish Sea scorpibum S
bumfish Sea scorpibum Spiny bum-urchin Oct
pibum Spiny bum-urchin Octostenchosaurus Bum
in Octostenchosaurus Bum-sponge Trilobut
ostenchosaurus Bum-sponge Trilobutt Jelly bumf
-sponge Trilobutt Jelly bumfish Sea scorpibum S
bumfish Sea scorpibum Spiny bum-urchin Oct
pibum Spiny bum-urchin Octostenchosaurus Bum
in Octostenchosaurus Bum-sponge Trilobut
ostenchosaurus Bum-sponge Trilobutt Jelly bumf
-sponge Trilobutt Jelly bumfish Sea scorpibum S
bumfish Sea scorpibum Spiny bum-urchin Oct
pibum Spiny bum-urchin Octostenchosaurus Bum
in Octostenchosaurus Bum-sponge Trilobut
ostenchosaurus Bum-sponge Trilobutt Jelly bumf
-sponge Trilobutt Jelly bumfish Sea scorpibum S
bumfish Sea scorpibum Spiny bum-urchin Oct
pibum Spiny bum-urchin Octostenchosaurus Bum
in Octostenchosaurus Bum-sponge Trilobut
ostenchosaurus Bum-sponge Trilobutt Jelly bumf
-sponge Trilobutt Jelly bumfish Sea scorpibum S
bumfish Sea scorpibum Spiny bum-urchin Oct

ge Trilobutt Jelly bumfish Sea scorpibum Spiny b
Jelly bumfish Sea scorpibum Spiny bum-ur
Sea scorpibum Spiny bum-urchin Octostenchosa
bum-urchin Octostenchosaurus Bum-sponge Trilo
nchosaurus Bum-sponge Trilobutt Jelly bumfish

Invertebutts

Life on Earth began in the seas with primitive
bumteria during the Pre-crappian time. Over time,
these early single-cheeked bums clumped together
to form some of the first multi-cheeked
invertebutts in the Crapozoic era oceans.

BUM-SPONGE

TRILOBUTT

JELLY BUMFISH

SEA SCORPIBUM

SPINY BUM-URCHIN

OCTOBUMOPUS

nchosaurus Bum-sponge Trilobutt Jelly bumfish
nge Trilobutt Jelly bumfish Sea scorpibum Spiny b
Jelly bumfish Sea scorpibum Spiny bum-ur
Sea scorpibum Spiny bum-urchin Octostenchosa
bum-urchin Octostenchosaurus Bum-sponge Trilo
nchosaurus Bum-sponge Trilobutt Jelly bumfish

Bum-sponge

The Bum-sponge lived permanently attached to the sea floor, absorbing bumteria. It had two distinct cheeks, which is the identifying characteristic of all forms of bum life, both modern and prehistoric.

What it lacked, however, were arms, legs, a mouth, internal organs, a nervous system, a personality and hobbies or interests of any kind.

It is believed that the species was forced to bumvolve other features, such as the ability to create bubbles by releasing gas underwater, in an effort to entertain itself and relieve the boredom of its incredibly dull life.

VITAL STATISTICS

Scientific name: *Squeezius cheeki*
Family: Squisherbutt
Diet: Bumteria-ivorarse
Time: Crappian 540–500 mya
Stink rating: 🖤 🖤 🖤 🖤 🖤

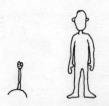

4

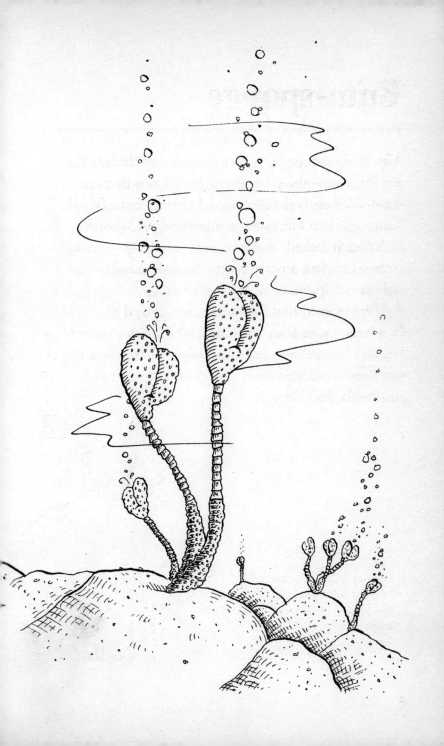

Trilobutt

Appearing some 600 million years ago, the Trilobutt was a hard, triple-cheeked bottom feeder. Its flattened shape made it uniquely suited to filtering mud, invertebutt droppings and bumganic particles as it scuttled along the sea floor.

Its hard shell kept it safe from predators; thus it was one of the most successful of all early bum life forms. It swam, crawled and burrowed in the Crapozoic oceans for the next 350 million years.

There were many different species of Trilobutt, and some – such as *Trilobuttus gigantis* – grew to enormarse proportions.

VITAL STATISTICS

Scientific name: *Tricheekium buttus*
Family: Stinkerbutt
Diet: Mudivorarse
Time: Crapozoic era 540–250 mya
Stink rating:

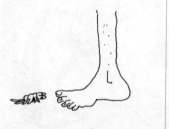

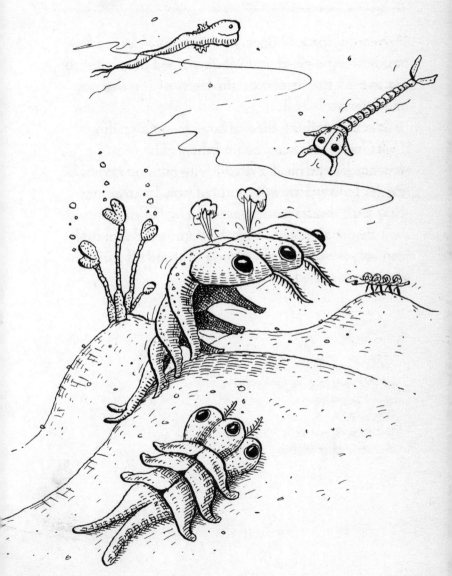

Jelly bumfish

Despite having no bones, no heart, no blood and no brains, the gas-filled, bumcheek-shaped Jelly bumfish was one of the fiercest of the later soft-bodied invertebutts.

Jelly bumfish travelled in large schools, trailing their long stenchtacles behind them. These stenchtacles each had a deadly jelly-bum on the end, which could swiftly kill captured prey by infecting them with deadly bumteria. The Jelly bumfish would then absorb the prey's body by bumosis, a primitive form of osmosis in which food is absorbed through tiny pores in the bum cheeks.

VITAL STATISTICS

Scientific name: *Piscatis jellibulus*
Family: Squisherbutt
Diet: Carnivorarse
Time: Ordungocian 500–435 mya
Stink rating:

Sea scorpibum

The Sea scorpibum was the giant ancestor of the modern-day scorpion, and one of the most feared prehistoric deep-water bum life forms. The enormous claws of a Sea scorpibum could cut a giant Trilobutt in half, and the venom-sacs in its bum-shaped stinger contained raw sewage so potent it could kill a school of Jelly bumfish within seconds.

Evidence suggests, however, that these terrifying creatures engaged in quite elegant courtship rituals. These would begin with the male grasping the female's pincers and performing a dance called the *bumenade a deux*. This dance eventually developed into a range of styles, including bumroom dancing, bum-ballet, stench-jazz and stink-hop.

VITAL STATISTICS

Scientific name: *Scorpius oceania*
Family: Pinchabutt
Diet: Carnivorarse
Time: Ordungocian, Sewerian 500–410 mya
Stink rating: 🏵🏵 🏵 🏵 🏵

Spiny bum-urchin

One of the spikiest and most unpleasant of the unpleasant prehistoric deep-water creatures, the Spiny bum-urchin left behind a trail of death and destruction wherever it went.

Although it fed exclusively on other smaller Spiny bum-urchins (stuffing them two or three at a time into its horrid little spiny mouth), many other creatures were spiked to death on its long spiny spines as it moved across the prehistoric ocean floor in search of more Spiny bum-urchins to stuff into its horrid little spiny mouth.

VITAL STATISTICS

Scientific name: *Spinius bumi*
Family: Cannibalobutt
Diet: Spiny bum-urchinivorarse
Time: Ordungocian 500–435 mya
Stink rating:

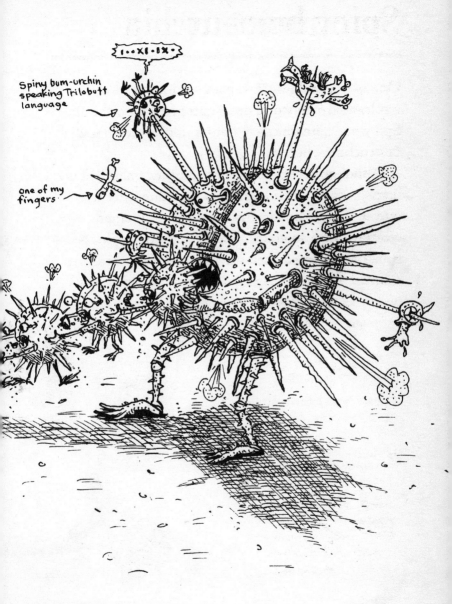

13

Octobumopus

The eight-armed, eight-headed, sixteen-cheeked, sixteen-eyed Octobumopus was a predecessor of the eight-armed, one-headed, two-eyed octopus that we are familiar with today.

As well as being bizarre in appearance, the Octobumopus had a highly developed defence system. If threatened, it would eject eight clouds of thick brownish liquid to blind – and disgust – predators. It would then use the incredible thrusting power of its sixteen cheeks to escape at high speed, leaving its attacker completely grossed out and in desperate need of an industrial-strength disinfectant.

VITAL STATISTICS

Scientific name: *Octavio posteriosi*
Family: Freakasaur
Diet: Carnivorarse
Time: Sewerian 435–410 mya
Stink rating:

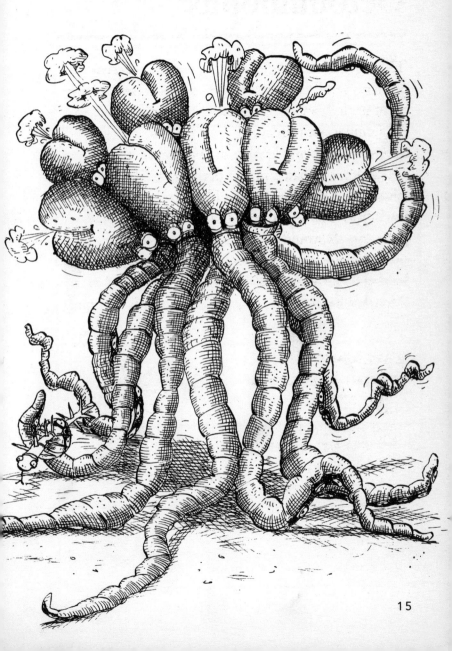

Bumolutionary time-chart

PRE-CRAPPIAN TIME
4600–540 million years ago (mya)
Origin of bum life in the sea

CRAPOZOIC ERA

CRAPPIAN PERIOD
540–500 mya
First invertebutts

ORDUNGOCIAN PERIOD
500–435 mya
First vertebutts (bumfish) and bum-plants

SEWERIAN PERIOD
435–410 mya
Armoured bumfish

DEBUMIAN PERIOD
410–355 mya
First bumphibians

CARBUMIFEROUS PERIOD
355–295 mya
First stinksects and farthropods

POOMIAN PERIOD
First stenchtiles
295–250 mya

MESSOZOIC ERA

TRIARSSIC PERIOD
First bumosaurs
250–203 mya

JURARSSIC PERIOD
First flying bumosaurs
203–135 mya

CRAPACEOUS PERIOD
135–65 mya
First gigantic bumosaurs

SCENTOZOIC ERA

FARTOCENE EPOCH
65–1.75 mya
First bummals

BUMOCENE EPOCH
1.75 mya –present
First Bumanderthals and bum-men

ray Stinkleosteus Bum-head shark Deep-sea h
kleosteus Bum-head shark Deep-sea bum-dangler
-head shark Deep-sea bum-dangler Brown-blobped
-sea bum-dangler Brown-blobpedo fish Colonaca
ler Brown-blobpedo fish Colonacanth Bumray St
pedo fish Colonacanth Bumray Stinkleosteus Bi
nacanth Bumray Stinkleosteus Bum-head shark
ray Stinkleosteus Bum-head shark Deep-sea h
kleosteus Bum-head shark Deep-sea bum-dangler
-head shark Deep-sea bum-dangler Brown-blobped
-sea bum-dangler Brown-blobpedo fish Colonaca
ler Brown-blobpedo fish Colonacanth Bumray St
pedo fish Colonacanth Bumray Stinkleosteus Bi
nacanth Bumray Stinkleosteus Bum-head shark
ray Stinkleosteus Bum-head shark Deep-sea h
kleosteus Bum-head shark Deep-sea bum-dangler
-head shark Deep-sea bum-dangler Brown-blobpec
-sea bum-dangler Brown-blobpedo fish Colonaca
ler Brown-blobpedo fish Colonacanth Bumray S
pedo fish Colonacanth Bumray Stinkleosteus Bi
nacanth Bumray Stinkleosteus Bum-head shark
ray Stinkleosteus Bum-head shark Deep-sea h
kleosteus Bum-head shark Deep-sea bum-dangler
-head shark Deep-sea bum-dangler Brown-blobpec
-sea bum-dangler Brown-blobpedo fish Colonaca
ler Brown-blobpedo fish Colonacanth Bumray S
pedo fish Colonacanth Bumray Stinkleosteus Bi
nacanth Bumray Stinkleosteus Bum-head shark
ray Stinkleosteus Bum-head shark Deep-sea l
kleosteus Bum-head shark Deep-sea bum-dangler

Bumfish

Major advances in bumolution during the Crapozoic era saw the rise of the first vertebutts (bum life forms with internal skeletons). During the Ordungocian period (500–435 million years ago) the first bumfish appeared and soon bumvolved into an astonishing variety of forms that quickly came to dominate the prehistoric seas.

BROWN-BLOBPEDO FISH
COLONACANTH
BUMRAY
STINKLEOSTEUS
BUM-HEAD SHARK
DEEP-SEA BUM-DANGLER

Brown-blobpedo fish

The Brown-blobpedo fish was one of the earliest bum life forms to use brown blobs – self-propelled, cigar-shaped missiles – as a means of attack and defence.

The Brown-blobpedo fish launched these brown blobs, or blobpedoes, at any creature unfortunate enough to stray into its territory, usually with predictably devarsetating results.

Successive generations of Brown-blobpedo fish developed the ability to equip their blobpedoes with homing devices and explosive heads. The Brown-blobpedo fish eventually became exstinkt because its blobpedoes achieved such explosive power that they often detonated on launch and bumbliterated the Brown-blobpedo fish itself.

VITAL STATISTICS

Scientific name: *Blobpedis rancidius*
Family: Crapofish
Diet: Needle kelpivorarse
Time: Ordungocian, Sewerian 500–410 mya
Stink rating: 🖤🖤🖤🖤🖤

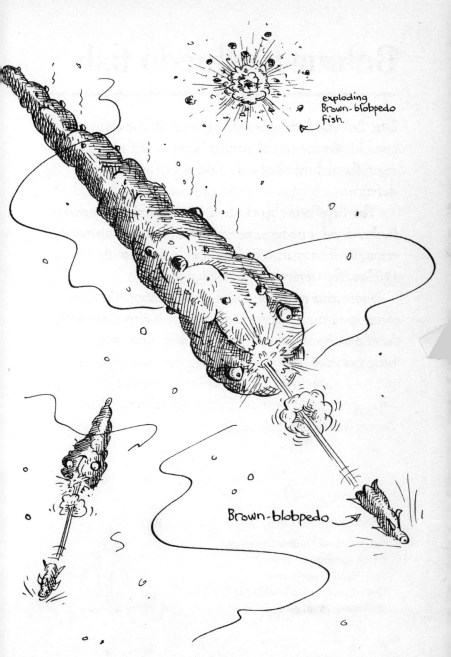

exploding
Brown-blobpedo
fish.

Brown-blobpedo →

21

Colonacanth

The Colonacanth appeared around 500 million years ago and was a close relative of one of the oldest living fossil fish, the Coelacanth (see inset). Little more than a length of intestine, the Colonacanth had few defences apart from its ability to startle potential predators with its ugly bum-shaped face. Unfortunately, many of these predators had ugly bum-shaped faces as well, so this defence was of limited value.

It also proved to be a serious handicap when trying to attract a mate. As a result of both of these disadvantages, the Colonacanth died out fairly quickly.

VITAL STATISTICS

Scientific name: *Colonic contagium*
Family: Ickyafish
Diet: Pooivorarse
Time: Ordungocian 500–435 mya
Stink rating: 💩💩💩💩💩

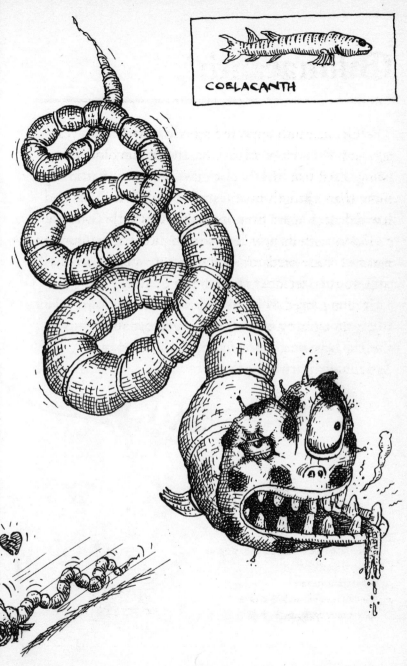

COELACANTH

Bumray

While stingrays today are mostly feared for the poisoned barbs on their tails, the Bumray was feared for its terrible breath, one blast of which was strong enough to kill a whole forest of needle kelp or reduce an Octobumopus to a puddle of brown jelly.

Occasionally, usually when frightened, the Bumray would emit breath so strong that it would blast itself up out of the water and have to use its aerobumnamic shape to glide safely back down again. It is thought by many bumosaurologists that this might have been one way in which bumosaurs eventually learned to fly.

razor-sharp barbs

VITAL STATISTICS

Scientific name: *Halitosis horrendous*
Family: Stenchafish
Diet: Herbivorarse
Time: Sewerian 435–410 mya
Stink rating: ✿✿✿✿✿

Bumray using bad breath to blast itself out of water

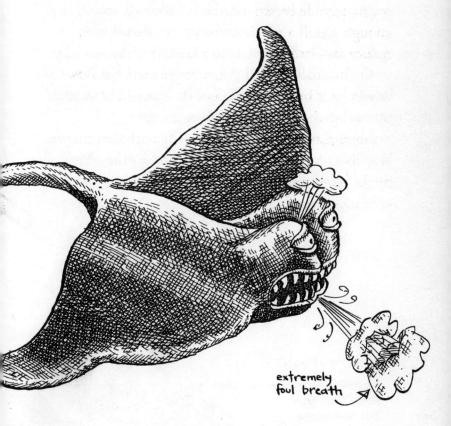

extremely
foul breath

Stinkleosteus

Stinkleosteus was enormarse, and one of the first armoured bumfish to bumvolve. Its bony plating protected it from the powerful pincers of such predators as the Sea scorpibum, and also shielded it against the withering effects of the Bumray's lethally smelly breath. Its third eye proved to be of great benefit in spotting – and thus avoiding – the deadly brown blobs fired by the Brown-blobpedo fish.

An undisputed ruler of the oceans, the enormarse, heavily armoured Stinkleosteus thrived throughout the Sewerian period.

VITAL STATISTICS

Scientific name: *Stinki indestructiblus*
Family: Squisherfish
Diet: Omnivorarse
Time: Sewerian 435–410 mya
Stink rating: 🐾🐾🐾🐾🐾

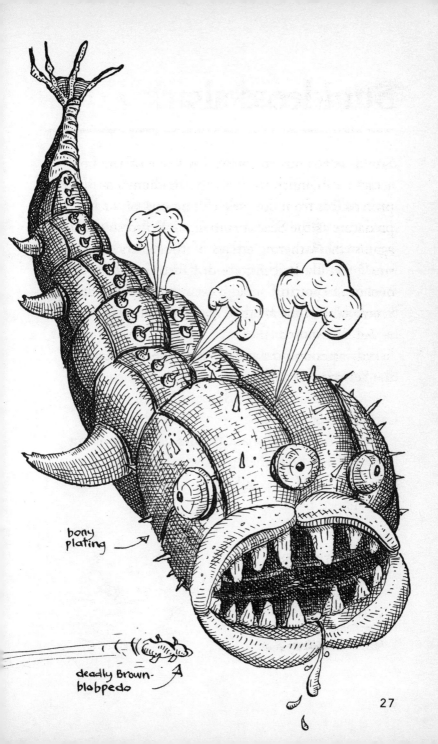

bony
plating →

deadly Brown-
blobpedo

Bum-head shark

A close relative of the better known – and still existing – Hammer-head shark, the Bum-head shark suffered from very low self-esteem due to the fact that everyone called it a bum-head. Which was true, but nevertheless very hurtful. For instance, how would you like it if everybody called *you* a bum-head? It would be hurtful enough even if you didn't have a bum-head . . . but imagine how much more it would hurt if you did.

It was perhaps the hurtful nature of this taunt that accounted for the extraordinary frequency and severity of Bum-head shark attacks during the Carbumiferous period.

So the Bum-head shark teaches us an important lesson: be kind to others . . . even if they act like bum-heads, and especially if they do have a bum-shaped head.

VITAL STATISTICS

Scientific name: *Bum-headius maximus*
Family: Bumshark
Diet: Carnivorarse
Time: Carbumiferous 355–295 mya
Stink rating: 🐾🐾🐾🐾🐾

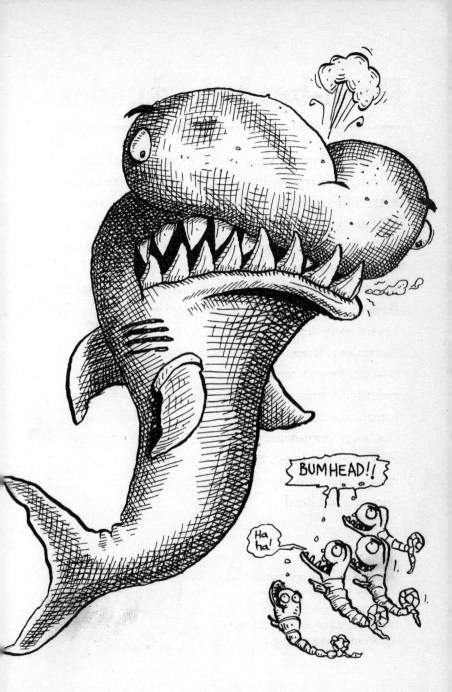

29

Deep-sea bum-dangler

The Deep-sea bum-dangler got its name from the
bioluminescent bum that dangled from its dorsal
spine. Millions of light-producing bumteria caused
this false bum to glow a blue-green colour. These
colourful lures came in a variety of styles and no two
were the same. Some had flashing pimples; others
had warts capable of impressive strobe-lighting
effects.

The Deep-sea bum-dangler used its false bum to
attract prey. It would wiggle the false bum in front of
its large, fang-packed mouth. Then, when its
fascinated, almost hypnotized, prey moved close
enough, the Deep-sea bum-dangler would flick its
dangling bum out of the way and snap up the prey
in its powerful jaws.

VITAL STATISTICS

Scientific name: *Dangleri prosthetica*
Family: Freakafish
Diet: Bumfishivorarse
Time: Carbumiferous 355–295 mya
Stink rating: ✿✿✿✿✿

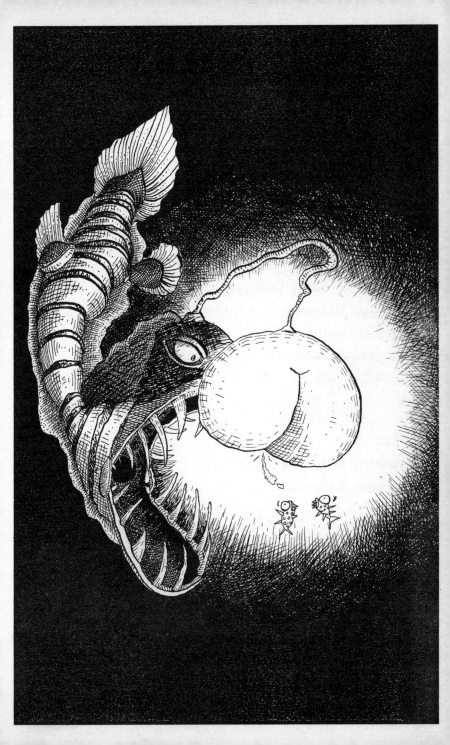

Bumolution: how life bumvolved

Life on Earth began with bumteria that appeared in the oceans 600 million years ago. Over time, these bumteria bumvolved into more complex forms of bum life until eventually giving rise to the group of stenchtiles we know as the bumosaurs. The exstinktion of the bumosaurs around 65 million years ago allowed a new species of bum life called bummals to bumvolve, eventually leading to the emergence of the earliest bum-men.

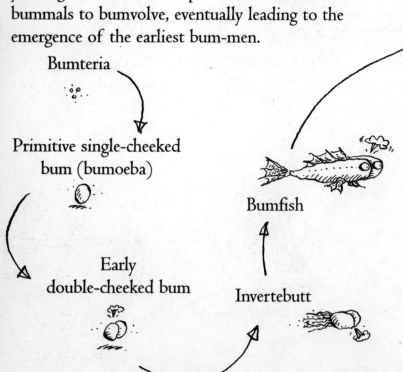

Bumteria

Primitive single-cheeked bum (bumoeba)

Bumfish

Early double-cheeked bum

Invertebutt

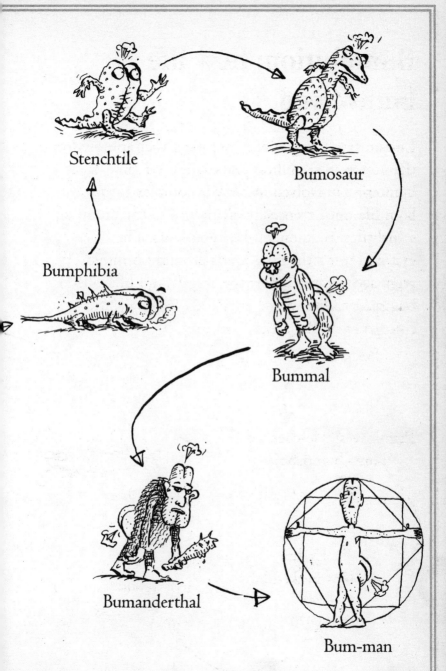

Stenchtile

Bumosaur

Bumphibia

Bummal

Bumanderthal

Bum-man

osaurus Turdle Bumaconstrictor Bumskipper Bo
aconstrictor Bumskipper Bogasaurus Bumetrodon Po
saurus Bumetrodon Poopigator Scatosaurus Turdl
pigator Scatosaurus Turdle Bumaconstrictor Bumskipp
aconstrictor Bumskipper Bogasaurus Bumetrodon Poo
saurus Bumetrodon Poopigator Scatosaurus Turdle
pigator Scatosaurus Turdle Bumaconstrictor Bumskipp
aconstrictor Bumskipper Bogasaurus Bumetrodon Poo
saurus Bumetrodon Poopigator Scatosaurus Turdle
pigator Scatosaurus urdle Bumaconstrictor Bumskippe
aconstrictor Bumskipper Bogasaurus Bumetrodon Poo
saurus Bumetrodon Poopigator Scatosaurus Turdle
pigator Scatosaurus Turdle Bumaconstrictor Bumskipp
aconstrictor Bumskipper Bogasaurus Bumetrodon Poo
saurus Bumetrodon Poopigator Scatosaurus Turdle
pigator Scatosaurus Turdle Bumaconstrictor Bumskipp
aconstrictor Bumskipper Bogasaurus Bumetrodon Poo
saurus Bumetrodon Poopigator Scatosaurus Turdle
pigator Scatosaurus Turdle Bumaconstrictor Bumskipp
aconstrictor Bumskipper Bogasaurus Bumetrodon Poo
saurus Bumetrodon Poopigator Scatosaurus Turdle
pigator Scatosaurus Turdle Bumaconstrictor Bumskipp
aconstrictor Bumskipper Bogasaurus Bumetrodon Poo
saurus Bumetrodon Poopigator Scatosaurus Turdle
pigator Scatosaurus Turdle Bumaconstrictor Bumskipp
aconstrictor Bumskipper Bogasaurus Bumetrodon Poo
saurus Bumetrodon Poopigator Scatosaurus Turdl
pigator Scatosaurus Turdle Bumaconstrictor Bumskipj
aconstrictor Bumskipper Bogasaurus Bumetrodon Poo
saurus Bumetrodon Poopigat Scatosaurus Turdle

aurus Bumetrodon Poopigator Scatosaurus Tu
igator Scatosaurus Turdle Bumaconstrictor Bumskip
Bumaconstrictor Bumskipper Bogasaurus Bumetro
Boga Tu
gator skip
mac etro
Boga Tu
gator skip
mac etro
Boga Tu
gator skip
mac etro
Boga Tu
gator skip
mac etro
Boga Tu
gator skip
mac etro
Boga Tu
gator skip
mac etro
Boga Tu
gator skip

Bumphibians
& Stenchtiles

Around 400 million years ago, using their fins as
primitive limbs, some of the more adventurous
bumfish crawled on to land to take up residence in
the abundant swamps and bogs of the Crapozoic era.
The descendants of these brave pooineers bumvolved
into the first bumphibians and then stenchtiles.

BUMSKIPPER
BOGASAURUS
BUMETRODON
POOPIGATOR
SCATOSAURUS
TURDLE
BUMACONSTRICTOR

Bumaconstrictor Bumskipper Bogasaurus Bumetro
Bogasaurus Bumetrodon Poopigator Scatosaurus Tu
igator Scatosaurus Turdle Bumaconstrictor Bumskip
umaconstrictor Bumskipper Bogasaurus Bumetro

Bumskipper

The Bumskipper was one of the first true bumphibians, able to live both in and out of the water. On land the Bumskipper moved along the bog shores by 'skipping' on its bum-shaped fins.

Living on land gave the Bumskipper tremendous advantages, the most important of which was the ability to release gas in private without the embarrassing telltale bubbles that accompany it in water. Of course, releasing gas above water meant the noises that often accompany the action could be heard clearly for the first time. These noises, however, were deemed so amusing that the Bumskipper was happy to give up its recently won privacy, and rapidly developed the full range of expressive sound effects that bums still employ – and enjoy so much – today.

VITAL STATISTICS

Scientific name: *Tetratis poddus*
Family: Stinkophibian
Diet: Herbivorarse
Time: Debumian 410–355 mya
Stink rating: ✿✿✿✿✿✿

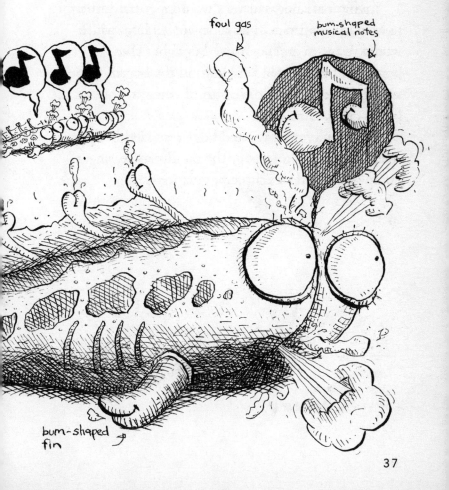

foul gas

bum-shaped
musical notes

bum-shaped
fin

Bogasaurus

The Bogasaurus, as its name suggests, was generally found in a bog. These huge, brown, particularly foul-smelling bogs were created by the male Bogasaurus in order to attract a female, known as a Bogasauress.

Young male Bogasauruses would regularly attempt to take up residence in an older male's bog, which would result in an enormarse bogfight. These bogfights could extend far beyond the bog in dispute and ended only with the death of one – or often both – Bogasauruses.

Meanwhile, their vacated bogs provided living space and nourishment for the rapidly increasing bumphibian and stenchtile populations.

VITAL STATISTICS

Scientific name: *Bogassius bogi*
Family: Crapophibian
Diet: Bogivorarse
Time: Carbumiferous 355–295 mya
Stink rating: ✿✿✿✿✿

Bumetrodon

Bumetrodon featured a bum-shaped 'sail' rising from its back. This sail was made up of ten hollow spines and covered in thick pink skin.

There is much speculation about the purpose of this sail. Some bumosaurologists think that the hollow spines served as 'chimneys', which helped to release the excess gases caused by the Bumetrodon's almost exclusive diet of stinkants.

Other bumosaurologists believe that the Bumetrodon's sail was intended to make its bum appear much bigger than it actually was in order to scare away predators.

Scientific name: *Buttus sailius*
Family: Stinkotile
Diet: Stinkantivorarse, Bogivorarse
Time: Poomian 295–250 mya
Stink rating:

Poopigator

The Poopigator bore a strong resemblance to the modern alligator, only it was much bigger, much browner and much, much smellier. While its appearance was quite threatening, the Poopigator's breath was far worse than its bite. Nevertheless, its bite was still quite bad.

The Poopigator consumed large prey by dragging it into a bog and then spinning or convulsing wildly until bite-size pieces were torn off. This is referred to as the 'deathbog roll' – not to be confused with 'bog roll', which is slang for toilet paper.

VITAL STATISTICS

Scientific name: *Poopius gatori*
Family: Crapotile
Diet: Omnivorarse, Bogivorarse
Time: Poomian 295–250 mya
Stink rating: 💩💩💩💩💩

Scatosaurus

Scatosaurus was one of the earliest stenchtiles to appear on Earth. These large, lizard-like creatures had tough, scaly skins that stopped their cheeks from drying out and were therefore able to live exclusively on land.

Stenchtiles were so named because their diet always consisted of bog, which gave them their distinctive – and very strong – 'stench'.

Scatosaurus made the most of this feature by using its stench as a means of defence. If threatened, it would inflate its expandable cheek sacs to ten times their normal size and then release an overpowering cloud of foul-smelling odour.

These cheek displays also may have been used by males in courting rituals, the odour in this case serving as a primitive perfume, irresistible to the female Scatosaurus.

VITAL STATISTICS

Scientific name: *Scatius maximius*
Family: Stinkotile
Diet: Bogivorarse
Time: Poomian 295–250 mya
Stink rating: 🐾🐾🐾🐾🐾

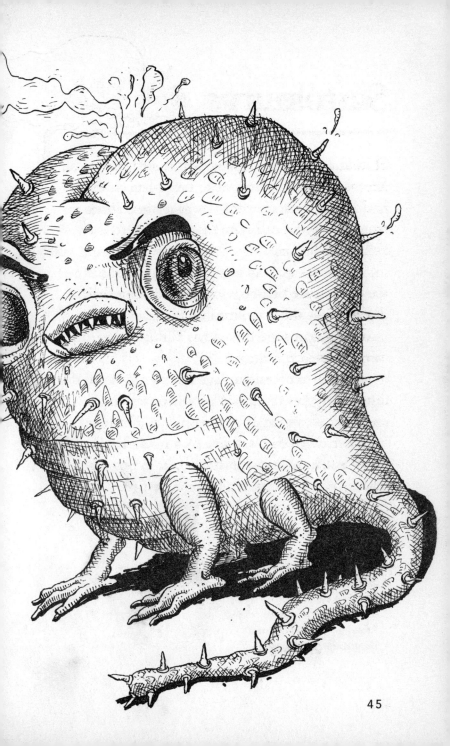

Turdle

The Turdle was the slowest and most timid of all stenchtiles and is thought to be a predecessor of modern tortoises and turtles as it has features in common with both species.

At the first sign of danger the Turdle would pull in its arms, legs, neck and head so it would appear to be just a piece of poo, virtually indistinguishable from all the other millions of pieces of poo on the ground . . . or were they other Turdles engaged in a similar defence strategy?

This form of camouflage was so successful that often a Turdle would not be able to tell the difference between a piece of poo and a fellow member of its own species. As a result Turdles would often make the tragic mistake of selecting a poo rather than a Turdle as a lifetime partner.

VITAL STATISTICS

Scientific name: *Turdi domesticus*
Family: Turdotile
Diet: Herbivorarse, Bogivorarse
Time: Triarssic 250–203 mya
Stink rating: ✿✿✿✿✿

Bumaconstrictor

Easily the longest of all known stenchtiles, the Bumaconstrictor lived a dreary and unpleasant life dragging its super-stretched buttocks through the bog and dung that covered 99.99999% of the Earth's surface during the Messozoic era.

A brutal hunter, the Bumaconstrictor liked to wrap its extraordinarily elongated cheeks around its victim and squeeze it to death before swallowing it whole.

One of the Bumaconstrictor's favourite foods was the Toiletbrushasaurus, and it was capable of devouring a complete herd of these hardworking creatures during a single hunt. Unfortunately, the Bumaconstrictor's Toiletbrushasaurus-binges only served to worsen the condition of the prehistoric bumvironment and make things even more unpleasant for itself.

VITAL STATISTICS

Scientific name: *Lengthius cheeki*
Family: Freakatile
Diet: Toiletbrushasauruses, Bogivorarse
Time: Messozoic era 250–65 mya
Stink rating: 💩💩💩💩💩

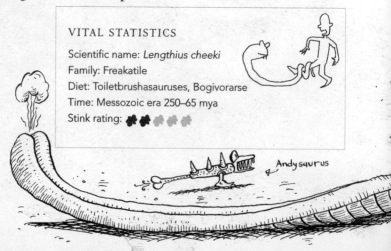

Andysaurus

Prehistoric bum-plant life

The first plants appeared in the abundant warm cracks and bogs of the Ordungocian period. By the end of the Debumian, plants were flourishing in almost every habitat on Earth and were every bit as rich, varied and smelly as the bum-related life forms that fed on them.

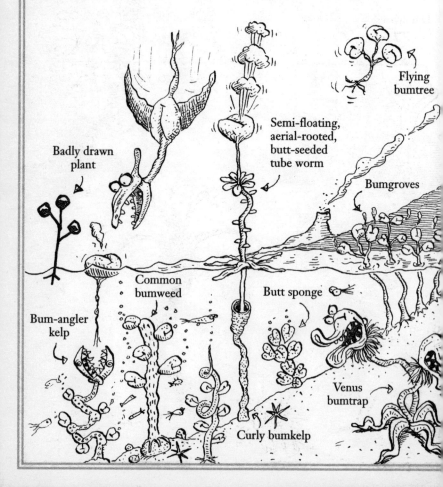

Flying bumtree

Badly drawn plant

Semi-floating, aerial-rooted, butt-seeded tube worm

Bumgroves

Common bumweed

Butt sponge

Bum-angler kelp

Venus bumtrap

Curly bumkelp

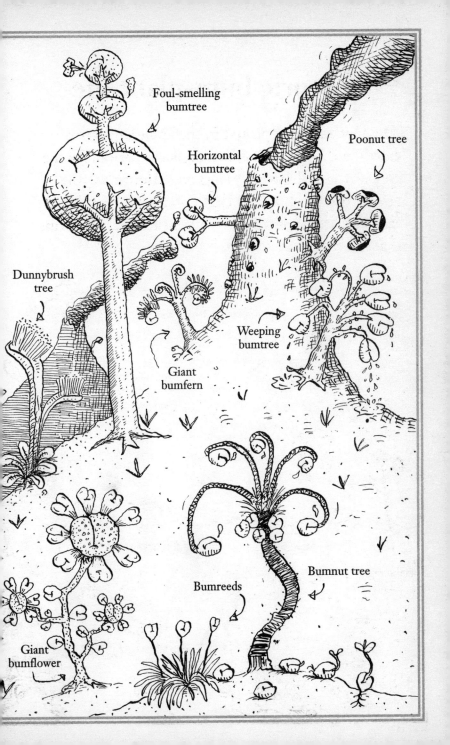

ant Blowfly Bumantula Giant Prehistoric Stinka
antula Giant Prehistoric Stinkant Bumipede Bur
istoric Stinkant Bumipede Bumslug Bumsquito C
ipede Bumslug Bumsquito Giant Mutant Blowfly
squito Giant Mutant Blowfly Bumantula Giant
ant Blowfly Bumantula Giant Prehistoric Stinka
antula Giant Prehistoric Stinkant Bumipede Bur
istoric Stinkant Bumipede Bumslug Bumsquito C
ipede Bumslug Bumsquito Giant Mutant Blowfly
squito Giant Mutant Blowfly Bumantula Giant
ant Blowfly Bumantula Giant Prehistoric Stinka
antula Giant Prehistoric Stinkant Bumipede Bur
istoric Stinkant Bumipede Bumslug Bumsquito C
ipede Bumslug Bumsquito Giant Mutant Blowfly
squito Giant Mutant Blowfly Bumantula Giant
ant Blowfly Bumantula Giant Prehistoric Stinka
antula Giant Prehistoric Stinkant Bumipede Bur
istoric Stinkant Bumipede Bumslug Bumsquito C
ipede Bumslug Bumsquito Giant Mutant Blowfly
squito Giant Mutant Blowfly Bumantula Giant
ant Blowfly Bumantula Giant Prehistoric Stinka
antula Giant Prehistoric Stinkant Bumipede Bur
istoric Stinkant Bumipede Bumslug Bumsquito C
ipede Bumslug Bumsquito Giant Mutant Blowfly
squito Giant Mutant Blowfly Bumantula Giant
ant Blowfly Bumantula Giant Prehistoric Stinka
antula Giant Prehistoric Stinkant Bumipede Bur
istoric Stinkant Bumipede Bumslug Bumsquito C
ipede Bumslug Bumsquito Giant Mutant Blowfly
squito Giant Mutant Blowfly Bumantula Giant

Farthropods & Stinksects

Hot on the heels of the bumphibians,
sea-dwelling invertebutts rapidly bumvolved
their own creeping, crawling, flying and
farting armies to invade the land.

BUMIPEDE

BUMSLUG

BUMSQUITO

GIANT MUTANT BLOWFLY

BUMANTULA

GIANT PREHISTORIC STINKANT

Bumipede

An early relative of the millipede and centipede families, the Bumipede had two thousand legs and one thousand bums, which made it very slow and very smelly. However, it was a strong burrower and its thousand-bum power made it very good at converting bumganic matter into rich bumus (or humus), a medium vital to the growth of healthy plants. The speed at which the Bumipede did this ensured the continuance of the cycle of fertility and, by extension, all bumosaur and bum-related life on Earth.

Unfortunately, the job of keeping its many bums clean was difficult for the Bumipede – its body was so long and so far behind that it was often in a different year or, in some extreme cases, a completely different century.

VITAL STATISTICS

Scientific name: *Millibumus leggus*
Family: Nauseopod
Diet: Dirtivorarse
Time: Carbumiferous 355–295 mya
Stink rating: ✿✿✿✿✿

slimy
decayed
bumnut

55

Bumslug

Truly deserving of its place in the Disgustapod family, the Bumslug did little but froth and burp and swear and gurgle and bubble and slime its way through the prehistoric landscape without so much as an 'excuse me' or a 'thank you'. Now, to be fair, the bumosaur world was hardly a place for fancy manners but, even so, the Bumslug really was a shocker. If another bum creature was foolish enough to get between the Bumslug and a can of Bumslug Beer, it would simply unleash a torrent of slimy mucarse and drown the unfortunate beast.

VITAL STATISTICS

Scientific name: *Frothus revolti*
Family: Disgustapod
Diet: Bumslug Beerivorarse
Time: Carbumiferous 355–295 mya
Stink rating: 🐾🐾🐾🐾

Bumsquito

The Bumsquito was similar to the modern mosquito, only much bigger, with many species growing to be the size of a light aircraft. Also unlike mosquitoes today, which will feed on any exposed part of a victim's body, the Bumsquito would attack only the bum of its prey. And a Bumsquito bite did not just leave a small, itchy red bump on the victim's skin either. In fact, a Bumsquito's victim often didn't have any skin left at all. Or flesh. Or blood. Or bones. Because the larger species of Bumsquito had the ability to suck its victim's entire body up through its enormarse bumboscis.

VITAL STATISTICS

Scientific name: *Bumboscius massiosius*
Family: Horribilosect
Diet: Bum-bloodivorarse
Time: Carbumiferous 355–295 mya
Stink rating: ♣ ♣ ♣ ♣ ♣

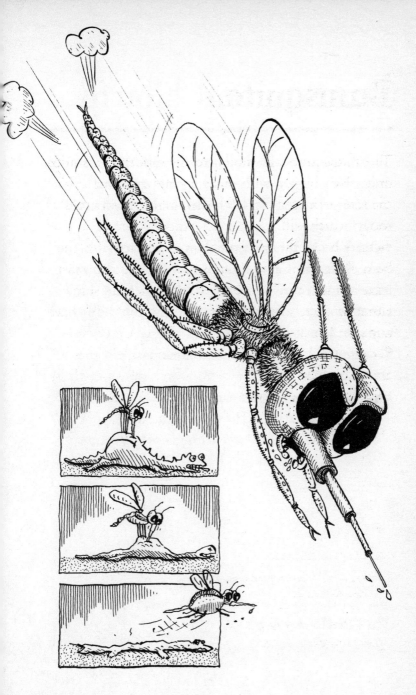

Giant mutant blowfly

While not technically a bumosaur itself, the Giant mutant blowfly was the constant companion of bumosaurs, thriving on both their waste products and their carcasses.

One million times bigger than its modern counterpart, the Giant mutant blowfly was also one million times more annoying. It liked to spray large quantities of yellowy-green goo out of its bumboscis, suck the head off its prey and lay Giant mutant maggots in the unfortunate victim's neck-hole.

While able to adapt successfully to any place where bumosaurs lived, the Giant mutant maggot grew especially gigantic in enclosed environments, such as bumcanoes and underground caves (also known as maggotoriums).

VITAL STATISTICS

Scientific name: *Mutatis blowflyus*
Family: Disgustosect
Diet: Omnivorarse
Time: Carbumiferous, Poomian, Triarssic 355–203 mya
Stink rating: 🟤🟤🟤⚪⚪

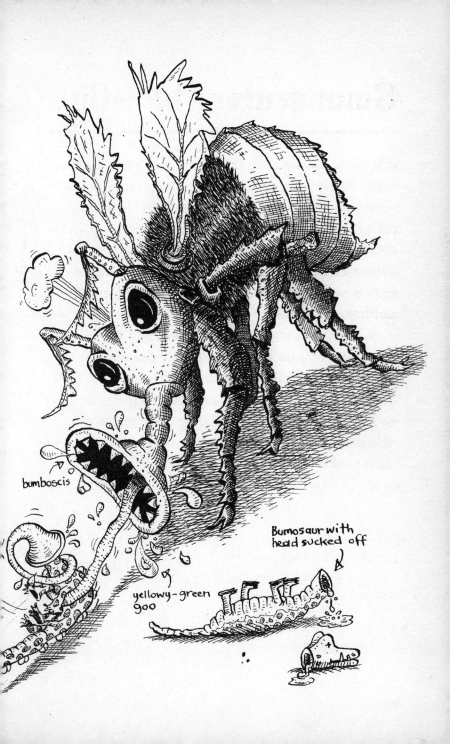

bumboscis

Bumosaur with
head sucked off

yellowy-green
goo

Bumantula

The Bumantula had an enormarse abdobum, eight beady brown eyes, two terrifying sharp fangs and eight powerful legs. The bum-web built by this prehistoric, spider-like Freakapod was made up of long brown strands of bum silk. These bum-webs were strong enough to catch large stinksects, as well as flying bumosaurs, such as Bumadactyls and Pteranobums.

While the Bumantula remained largely unchanged for almost 200 million years, the species did not exist in large numbers, due to the fact that most Bumantulas were scared of each other. And with good reason — attempts at mating often resulted in both Bumantulas crushing and stenching each other to death.

VITAL STATISTICS

Scientific name: *Posterius terribulus*
Family: Freakapod
Diet: Carnivorarse
Time: Messozoic era 250–65 mya
Stink rating:

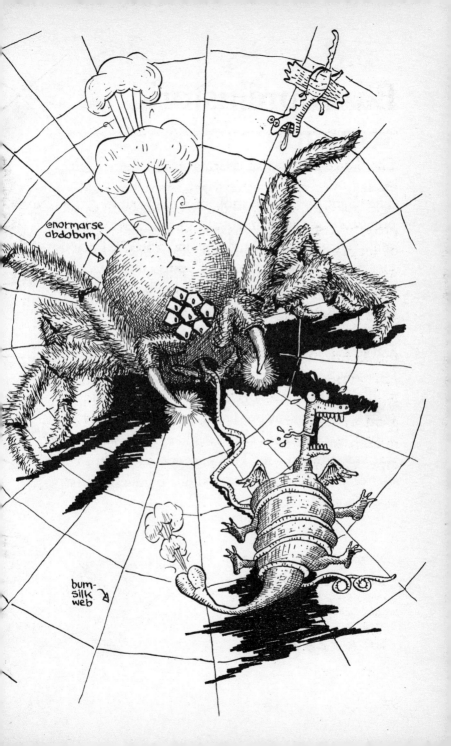

Giant prehistoric stinkant

The Giant prehistoric stinkant was a gigantic prehistoric ant with an equally gigantic prehistoric stink. It was generally bright red in colour, had vicious pincers and lived in colonies of up to 200,000.

The Giant prehistoric stinkant was highly sought after as a food source by some bumosaurs because eating the ant would usually result in terrible flatulence and serious body odour, which helped to increase a bumosaur's status in any herd's gassing order.

If squashed by a larger bumosaur, the Giant prehistoric stinkant produced huge quantities of a thick, greasy liquid called stinkant juice, which was excessively smelly. This juice was the exclusive diet of the Microbumosaurus, one of the smelliest of all bumosaurs.

VITAL STATISTICS

Scientific name: *Stinkantius giganti*
Family: Rancidosect
Diet: Carnivorarse
Time: Messozoic era 250–65 mya
Stink rating: 🐾🐾🐾🐾🐾

How a bumosaur works

From the outside, bumosaurs may
have appeared to be little more
than unpleasant loads of blubber,
gas and brown blobs.

The truth is, however,
that they were highly
complex loads of
blubber, gas and
brown blobs, as
the following
cutaway
diagram
clearly
demonstrates.

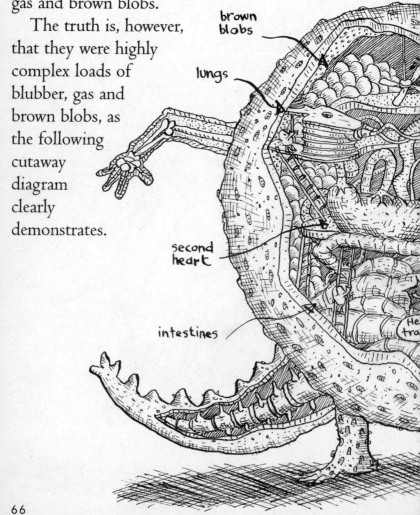

brown
blobs

lungs

second
heart

intestines

He
tra

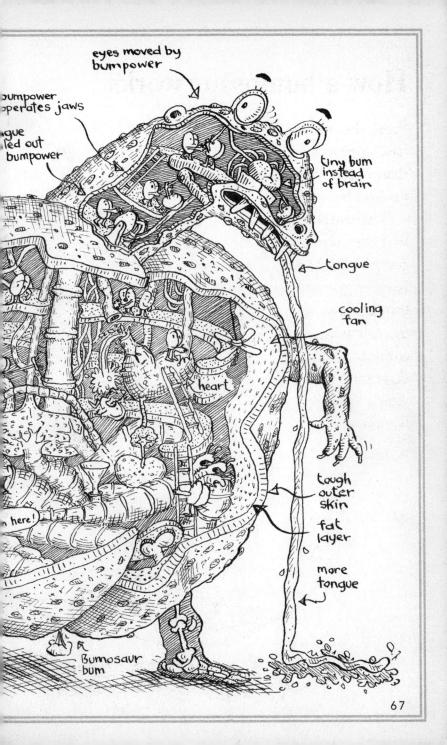

eyes moved by
bumpower

umpower
operates jaws

gue
led out
bumpower

tiny bum
instead
of brain

tongue

cooling
fan

heart

here!

tough
outer
skin

fat
layer

more
tongue

Bumosaur
bum

ersaurus Diarrhoeasaurus Itchybumosaurus Frill
k Kong Toiletbrushasaurus Tricerabutt Tyrannos
osaurus Microbumosaurus Stenchgantorsaurus Po
led idiotasaurus The very rare long-necked long-legg
asaurus Bum-eyed bumosaurus Bumontopinus D
opootops Skullbuttosaurus Sparebumosaurus Stink
rseosaurus Gigantarsesaurus Great white bumo
etrollasaurus Badlydrawn bumosaurus Bum-headed
d stupid-looking tiny bum-headed droopy-eyed
ersaurus Diarrhoeasaurus Itchybumosaurus Frill
k Kong Toiletbrushasaurus Tricerabutt Tyrannos
osaurus Microbumosaurus Stenchgantorsaurus Po
led idiotasaurus The very rare long-necked long-legg
asaurus Bum-eyed bumosaurus Bumontopinus D
opootops Skullbuttosaurus Sparebumosaurus Stink
rseosaurus Gigantarsesaurus Great white bumos
etrollasaurus Badlydrawn bumosaurus Bum-headed
d stupid-looking tiny bum-headed droopy-eyed
ersaurus Diarrhoeasaurus Itchybumosaurus Frill
k Kong Toiletbrushasaurus Tricerabutt Tyrannos
osaurus Microbumosaurus Stenchgantorsaurus Po
led idiotasaurus The very rare long-necked long-legg
asaurus Bum-eyed bumosaurus Bumontopinus Da
opootops Skullbuttosaurus Sparebumosaurus Stink
rseosaurus Gigantarsesaurus Great white bumos
etrollasaurus Badlydrawn bumosaurus Bum-headed
d stupid-looking tiny bum-headed droopy-eyed
ersaurus Diarrhoeasaurus Itchybumosaurus Frill
k Kong Toiletbrushasaurus Tricerabutt Tyrannos
osaurus Microbumosaurus Stenchgantorsaurus Po

Bumosaurs

The Messozoic era saw the rise of some of the best-known, most aggressive and most stupid members of the bumosaur family.

POOPASAUR

TOILETROLLASAURUS

BADLYDRAWN BUMOSAURUS

BUM-HEADED IDIOTASAURUS

VERY RARE LONG-NECKED LONG-LEGGED SHORT-TAILED
STUPID-LOOKING TINY BUM-HEADED DROOPY-EYED
IDIOTASAURUS

BUM-EYED BUMOSAURUS

BUMONTOPIMUS

DIAPERSAURUS

DIARRHOEASAURUS

ITCHYBUMOSAURUS

FRILL-NECKED CYCLOPOOTOPS

SKULLBUTTOSAURUS

SPAREBUMOSAURUS

STINK KONG

TOILETBRUSHASAURUS

TRICERABUTT

TYRANNOSORE-ARSE REX

BIGARSEOSAURUS

GIGANTARSESAURUS

GREAT WHITE BUMOSAURUS

MICROBUMOSAURUS

STENCHGANTORSAURUS

Poopasaur

The Poopasaur had brown skin, an enormarse mouth, small black eyes, sharp teeth, very bad breath and an even worse temper. It was well camouflaged for life in the swamps and primeval bumnut-tree forests and was prone to hiding in the undergrowth and then jumping out unexpectedly to catch its prey, which it would swallow in one gulp.

Unfortunately, its enormarse mouth was much bigger than its stomach and the Poopasaur would often overeat until it exploded.

The deadly brown clouds caused by these explosions – known as 'brown-outs' – made it impossible for other bumosaurs to see or breathe, and could last for several hours.

VITAL STATISTICS

Scientific name: *Crocodilius crappus*
Family: Craposaur
Diet: Omnivorarse
Time: Messozoic era 250–65 mya
Stink rating: ✿✿✿✿✿

exploding
Poopasaur →

Toiletrollasaurus

The Toiletrollasaurus appeared in a dazzling variety of colours, patterns and textures. Also known as the 'Bogrollasaurus', the various sub-species differed immensely in size, weight, tear-ability, softness, 'finger-breakthrough' resistance and degrees of absorption.

Despite these differences, they shared one common feature: a permanent expression of terror due to the fact that they were preyed upon by almost every other type of bumosaur. The Toiletrollasaurus was widely hunted because it was prized for its long, soft, absorbent tail. It is thought that the perforations on the Toiletrollasaurus's tail bumvolved as a defence against its many predators. Like some species of modern-day lizard, if caught by the tail it could lose a section and then regrow it.

VITAL STATISTICS

Scientific name: *Papyrus posteri*
Family: Wipeosaur
Diet: Herbivorarse
Time: Messozoic era 250–65 mya
Stink rating: 🌀🌀🌀🌀🌀

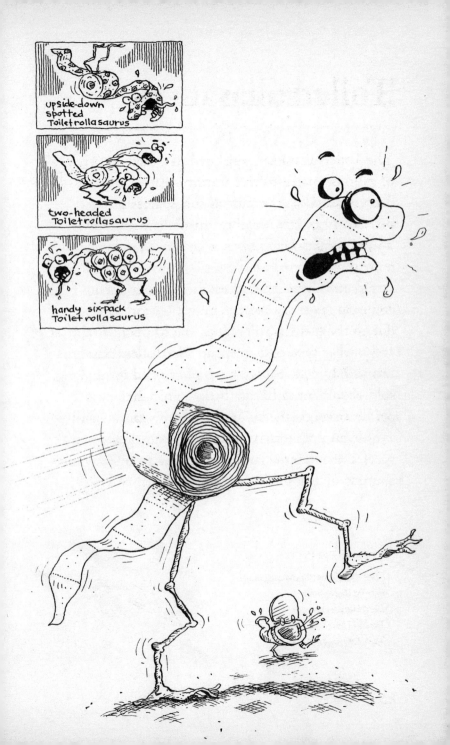

Badlydrawn bumosaurus

The most badly drawn of all the bumosaurs, Badlydrawn bumosaurus was the laughing stock of the bumosaur world. It was even looked down upon by the Bum-headed idiotasaurus which, although no pin-up itself, was drawn with at least a modicum of talent.

As a result of its low status, the Badlydrawn bumosaurus preferred to spend most of its time alone, feeding on badly drawn plants and drinking badly drawn water from a badly drawn lake next to a badly drawn bumcano under a badly drawn sun.

Though not attractive, it thrived during the age of the bumosaurs and can still be seen today in the work of children all over the world (see inset).

VITAL STATISTICS

Scientific name: *Craperi magnificus*
Family: Freakabutt
Diet: Badlydrawn plants
Time: Triarssic 250–203 mya
Stink rating: 🍀🍀🍀🍀🍀

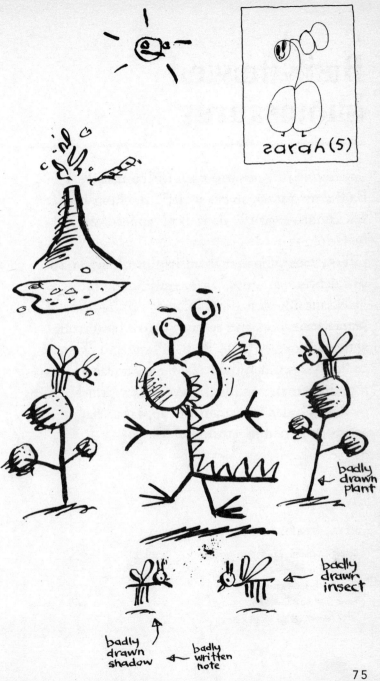

sarah (5)

badly
drawn
plant

badly
drawn
insect

badly
drawn
shadow

badly
written
note

Bum-headed idiotasaurus

Consisting of one large bum with a smaller bum-head atop a long, slug-like neck, the Bum-headed idiotasaurus was idiotic in both appearance and behaviour.

Like most idiots, it spent its time doing idiotic and dangerous things, such as swimming in quicksand-like bum-bogs, playing on the edges of active bumcanoes and running across busy roads without looking.

Not surprisingly, perhaps, bumosaurologists have found a number of fossil graveyards in which groups of Bum-headed idiotasauruses appear to have died and been buried together.

VITAL STATISTICS

Scientific name: *Dumbumius minor*
Family: Stupidosaur
Diet: Herbivorarse
Time: Triarssic 250–203 mya
Stink rating: 🌸🌸🌸🌸🌸

Very rare long-necked long-legged short-tailed stupid-looking tiny bum-headed droopy-eyed
idiotasaurus

The Very rare long-necked long-legged short-tailed stupid-looking tiny bum-headed droopy-eyed idiotasaurus was very rare due to the fact that it was too stupid to eat, drink, find shelter or even mate. If it did manage to reproduce, it was usually by accident.

In fact, the only interesting fact about the Very rare long-necked long-legged short-tailed stupid-looking tiny bum-headed droopy-eyed idiotasaurus is that it had the longest and stupidest-sounding name of all the bumosaurs.

VITAL STATISTICS

Scientific name: *Dumbumius major*
Family: Stupidosaur
Diet: Too dumb to eat
Time: Triarssic 250–203 mya
Stink rating:

Bum-eyed bumosaurus

Five eyes, six legs and twelve bum cheeks made the Bum-eyed bumosaurus one of the more bizarre and dangerous bumosaurs.

It could see in five directions at the same time and its six legs allowed it to cover vast distances very quickly. Its multiple cheeks also allowed it to produce five times as much gas as other similar-sized bumosaurs. It used this gas to stun its victims before eating them.

So the Bum-eyed bumosaurus was an excellent hunter and well protected from attack by other predators. In fact, the only creature the Bum-eyed bumosaurus had to fear was itself as it was very easy for a Bum-eyed bumosaurus to get its five necks in a knot and accidentally strangle itself to death.

VITAL STATISTICS

Scientific name: *Stupido stupendius*
Family: Freakabutt
Diet: Carnivorarse
Time: Triarssic 250–203 mya
Stink rating: 🐾🐾🐾🐾🐾

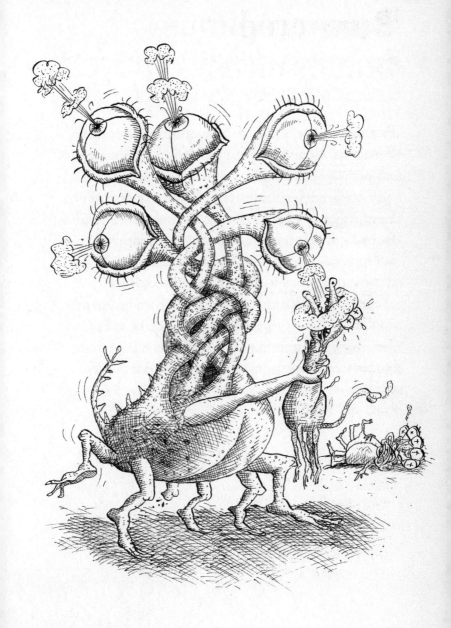

Bumontopimus

Bumontopimus spent most of its time stumbling around, holding its 'head' and trying to think of what to do next. This, of course, was impossible because its 'head' was in fact a bum, and as such it had no brain. The lack of a brain meant that it also had no memory, thus it often forgot that it had no brain, which is why it continued to spend so much of its time holding its 'head' and trying to think.

The sheer stupidity of the Bumontopimus made it an obvious target for any bumosaur looking for an easy meal and thus the species sadly became exstinkt quite soon after it first appeared. Not that it really mattered – Bumontopimuses were too stupid to know that they had even existed in the first place.

VITAL STATISTICS

Scientific name: *Butterius cranium*
Family: Stupidosaur
Diet: Can't remember to eat
Time: Triarssic 250–203 mya
Stink rating: 🐾🐾🐾

Diapersaurus

Coming in two main species, Cloth and Disposable, the small, highly intelligent Diapersaurus would attach itself to a new-born bumosaur of another species. This arrangement was beneficial to both parties. The Diapersaurus was provided with nourishment and protection from other large bumosaurs, and the young bumosaur was protected from the harsh conditions of the prehistoric bumosaur world.

These relationships were usually short-term, however, as the baby bumosaur would eventually outgrow the Diapersaurus and shed it, much like a snake sheds its skin. If it belonged to the Cloth species, the Diapersaurus would then move on and find a new host. If it belonged to the Disposable species, the Diapersaurus would die as soon as it was discarded.

Diapersaurus attaches itself to a newborn Bumosaur

Mature Bumosaur shedding its Diapersaurus

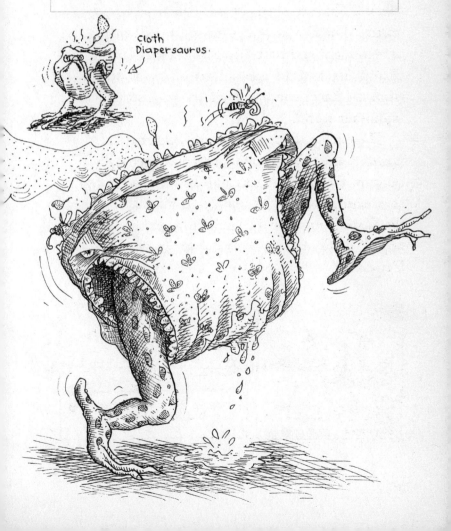

Cloth
Diapersaurus

Diarrhoeasaurus

Extremely unpleasant in both appearance and odour, the Diarrhoeasaurus also had one of the most unpleasant life-cycles of all bumosaurs.

Due to its runny consistency, Diarrhoeasaurus was unable to pick itself up off the ground and seek shelter from the hot Triarssic sun. This meant that it was usually baked hard within hours of being born and mistaken for a crunchy snack by another unsuspecting bumosaur. After eating the toxic Diarrhoeasaurus, this bumosaur would suffer horrible stomach pains, increased gas and terrible diarrhoea. Soon after, the Diarrhoeasaurus would be expelled from the sick bumosaur's body and deposited on the ground in its liquid form once more – ready to start its life-cycle over again.

VITAL STATISTICS

Scientific name: *Puddle detestabilis*
Family: Craposaur
Diet: Unknown
Time: Triarssic 250–203 mya
Stink rating: 💩💩💩💩💩

Itchybumosaurus

The Itchybumosaurus spent most of its time hopping around scratching itself.

It was covered in dry, chafed skin and often scratched itself so much that it scratched through its skin to the flesh below, leaving itself open to all manner of disgusting prehistoric bum infections. However, the dry skin that flaked off and fell to the ground was a rich source of nutrients for smaller bumosaurs, such as the Diapersaurus.

It was long thought that the only relief from itching for the Itchybumosaurus was death; however, there are many accounts from bumosaur museum curators of reconstructed Itchybumosaurus *bones* attempting to scratch themselves.

VITAL STATISTICS

Scientific name: *Itchi itchisori*
Family: Horribilosaur
Diet: Too busy scratching to eat
Time: Triarssic 250–203 mya
Stink rating: ✿✿✿✿✿

Frill-necked cyclopootops

Named after Cyclops, the legendary one-eyed giant, the Frill-necked cyclopootops was the most glamorous member of the bumosaur family. Its huge neck frill was both a defence mechanism – making it appear larger than it actually was – and a prehistoric fashion statement.

With its long curling eyelashes, rounded cheeks and painted toenails, the Frill-necked cyclopootops had a sense of beauty and style way ahead of its time.

Although it died out with the rest of the bumosaurs at the end of the Crapaceous period, the Frill-necked cyclopootops nevertheless has been admired and worshipped by many religions and cults throughout the last 65 million years.

VITAL STATISTICS

Scientific name: *Cyclopius amazingus*
Family: Freakabutt
Diet: Fashion magazines
Time: Jurarssic, Crapaceous 203–65 mya
Stink rating: ✿ ✿ ✿ ✿ ✿

pointy
things

Skullbuttosaurus

The Skullbuttosaurus was a nocturnal bumosaur and, when it wasn't engaged in violent skull-butting contests with rival Skullbuttosauruses, it could usually be found stalking the bumtree forests at night and using its alarming appearance to scare its prey to death. At the approach of a Skullbuttosaurus, other bumosaurs would spontaneously evacuate themselves or simply drop dead with fright.

Even gigantosaurs, such as the Bigarseosaurus and the Gigantarsesaurus, were scared of the Skullbuttosaurus. As a consequence, the Skullbuttosaurus always had an abundant food supply and became very widespread by the end of the Crapaceous period.

VITAL STATISTICS

Scientific name: *Cranium enormis*
Family: Horribilosaur
Diet: Carnivorarse
Time: Jurarssic, Crapaceous 203–65 mya
Stink rating: 🐾🐾🐾🐾🐾

Sparebumosaurus

A passive and comparatively peaceful bumosaur, the Sparebumosaurus gets its name from the row of miniature bums sticking up from its neck, back and tail. It is thought that these bums allowed the Sparebumosaurus to replace itself in the event of a fatal accident or attack.

If a Sparebumosaurus was killed, then any of the undamaged 'spare' bums could detach themselves and grow to become exact, fully formed replicas of the dead Sparebumosaurus. If any of these new Sparebumosauruses were killed too, then their spare bums could grow into perfect replicas and so on, effectively making the Sparebumosaurus virtually indestructible.

VITAL STATISTICS

Scientific name: *Replicus arsius*
Family: Stenchosaur
Diet: Herbivorarse
Time: Jurarssic, Crapaceous 203–65 mya
Stink rating: 🐾🐾🐾🐾🐾

rebirth of a
Sparebumosaurus

iature
ure
m

Stink Kong

This huge, gorilla-like bumosaur was covered in fur except for two bare patches on the front of each of its cheeks. These were caused by its habit of pounding on itself with its fists to produce a terrifying booming sound. This pounding also served to activate its numerous stench glands to produce a terrifying stink, hence its name.

Though resembling a gorilla in appearance, Stink Kong had little else in common with modern herbivorarse, herd-dwelling apes. Stink Kong was a clumsy, stupid, aggressive loner who liked nothing better than to get involved in violent brawls with any bumosaur willing to take it on. It and the Great white bumosaurus were natural enemies and often engaged in ferocious battles that lasted for many hours.

VITAL STATISTICS

Scientific name: *Fragrantus regis*
Family: Stinkosaur
Diet: Omnivorarse
Time: Jurarssic, Crapaceous 203–65 mya
Stink rating: 🐾🐾🐾🐾🐾

Toiletbrushasaurus

The Toiletbrushasaurus was the toilet cleaner of the prehistoric bumosaur world. Not that 'toilets' actually existed at the time – which is exactly why the Toiletbrushasaurus played such a vital role in prehistoric Earth's ecology.

Always in a hurry, the Toiletbrushasaurus moved quickly. As it did so, its many strong, bristly legs swept, cleaned and cleared the ground so that the rest of the bumosaurs actually had somewhere to walk instead of having to slosh around in their own ... well, let's just say that the average bumosaur produced up to 20 kilograms of it a day ... and there were a lot of bumosaurs ... which is probably why the Toiletbrushasaurus was always in such a hurry.

VITAL STATISTICS

Scientific name: *Bristilus lavatorum*
Family: Eeeuuw!osaur
Diet: Pooivorarse
Time: Jurarssic, Crapaceous 203–65 mya
Stink rating: 🐾🐾🐾🐾🐾

Tricerabutt

The Tricerabutt was a triple-cheeked bumosaur with bony armour plating and tusk-like wart-horns growing out of each of its cheeks.

Tricerabutts tended to form gangs of three, which would then spend most of their time running around looking for other gangs of Tricerabutts to attack and stab with their horns. Drive-by hornings were common, despite the fact that cars were not to be invented for at least another 135 million years.

The Tricerabutt was not overly bright. Fossilized Tricerabutt bones show that many Tricerabutts died after running into trees, getting their horns stuck and not being able to get them out again.

VITAL STATISTICS

Scientific name: *Tricerabuttius*
Family: Stupidosaur
Diet: Herbivorarse
Time: Jurarssic, Crapaceous 203–65 mya
Stink rating:

Tyrannosore-arse rex

There were few bumosaurs with a worse temper than the Tyrannosore-arse rex. Driven into wild rages by the pain in its gigantic aching cheeks, it would rampage through the prehistoric forest, leaving hundreds of other bumosaurs either gassed, brown-blobbified or completely flattened.

The funny thing – or not so funny if you happened to be a Tyrannosore-arse rex – was that these rampages only served to make it even sorer – and angrier – than before.

Some experts blame the Tyrannosore-arse rex and its destructive rages for the exstinktion of many species of small bumosaurs. Others just feel sorry for it. Only one thing is known for sure: Tyrannosore-arse rex had a really sore arse.

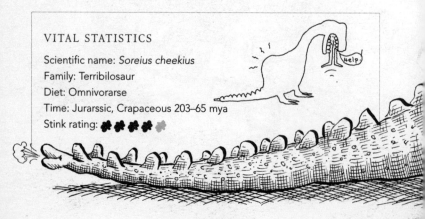

VITAL STATISTICS

Scientific name: *Soreius cheekius*
Family: Terribilosaur
Diet: Omnivorarse
Time: Jurarssic, Crapaceous 203–65 mya
Stink rating: ✿ ✿ ✿ ✿ ✿

Bigarseosaurus

The Bigarseosaurus was so named because of its incredibly big rear end. It was so big that every time Bigarseosaurus sat down it killed at least five other smaller bumosaurs. Despite this, it was a gentle but clumsy giant that lived on the juicy leaves and bumnuts from the tops of bumnut trees.

The rear end of the Bigarseosaurus continued to expand to increasingly alarming proportions throughout the Crapaceous period, and some bumosaurologists believe that the exstinktion of the bumosaurs was due to the Bigarseosauruses' big arses becoming so big that they blotted out the sun and plunged the Earth into an extended big-arse-induced winter.

VITAL STATISTICS

Scientific name: *Superio humungarse*
Family: Gigantosaur
Diet: Herbivorarse
Time: Crapaceous 135–65 mya
Stink rating: 🐾🐾🐾🐾🐾

Gigantarsesaurus

The largest of all of the bumosaurs, the Gigantarsesaurus was only on Earth for a comparatively brief time.

The creature was so heavy that when it walked it created giant cracks in the ground into which it would often fall.

The stupid little arms and feeble little legs of the Gigantarsesaurus were of no use for climbing so any that fell would then perish in these self-created 'cracks of doom'.

VITAL STATISTICS

Scientific name: *Superius gigantus*
Family: Gigantosaur
Diet: Omnivorarse
Time: Crapaceous 135–65 mya
Stink rating: 🐾🐾🐾🐾🐾

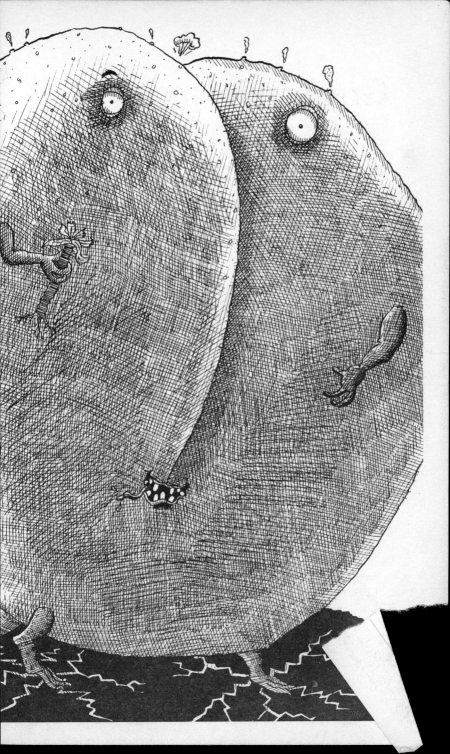

Great white bumosaurus

The Great white bumosaurus appeared on Earth towards the end of the late Crapaceous era. One of the truly gigantic bumosaurs, its most distinctive feature was its blindingly white skin. It is thought that this bioluminescence gave it a great advantage when fighting, as its incredible brightness could temporarily blind an opponent.

Some believe that the expression 'he/she thinks that the sun shines out of his/her behind' dates from the time that bumosaurologists first discovered fossil evidence of the Great white bumosaurus.

The Great white bumosaurus was also well known for its habit of dumping gigantic brown blobs on top of its enemies.

VITAL STATISTICS

Scientific name: *Maximus albinus*
Family: Disgustosaur
Diet: Omnivorarse
Time: Crapaceous 135–65 mya
Stink rating: 🐾🐾🐾🐾🐾

Microbumosaurus

The Microbumosaurus was the smallest of all known
bumosaurs, but it is classed as belonging to the
Gigantosaur family because of its massively putrid,
nostril-burning, nausea-inducing, eyebrow-singeing,
throat-gagging, lung-collapsing, migraine-making,
fever-causing, heart-stopping, blood-curdling,
eyeball-popping stink.

With this stink, which is thought to have been
caused by its exclusive diet of stinkant juice, it was
capable of knocking out – and sometimes even
killing – bumosaurs up to 100,000 times its size.

Small in stature, the Microbumosaurus was
nevertheless enormous in impact. Some experts even
speculate that the exstinktion of the bumosaurs may
have been caused by a sudden explosion in the
Microbumosaurus population.

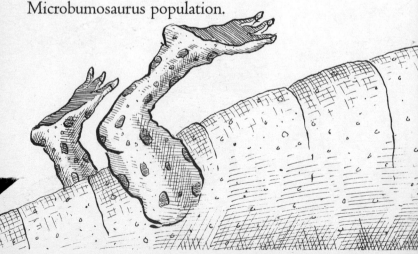

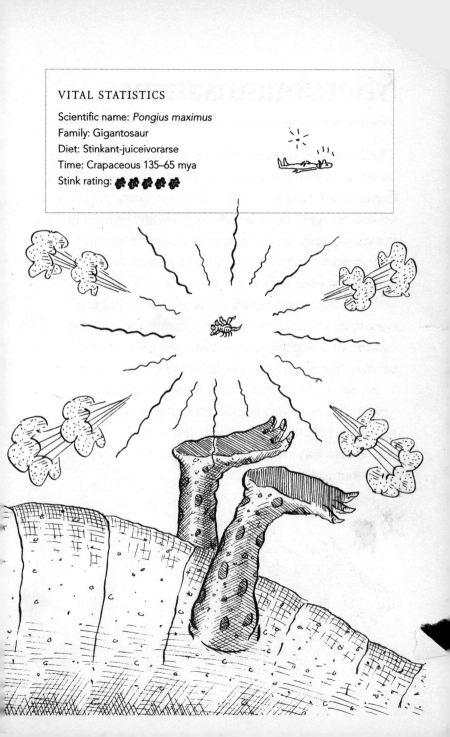

VITAL STATISTICS

Scientific name: *Pongius maximus*
Family: Gigantosaur
Diet: Stinkant-juiceivorarse
Time: Crapaceous 135–65 mya
Stink rating: 💩💩💩💩💩

tenchgantorsaurus

The Stenchgantorsaurus was one of the ugliest, dirtiest, wartiest, pimpliest, grossest, greasiest, hairiest and stinkiest of all the bumosaurs.

It is thought that it grew to be so disgusting because it lived such a long life – some specimens have been found that are thought to have had a life span of at least 400 years. And 400 years is a long time for a bum to go without being wiped. As a result, the Stenchgantorsaurus was completely blind and was one of the few bumosaurs to have a highly developed sense of smell, which it used to locate prey.

It was also prone to developing enormarse bum-pimples, which would often burst in spectacular fashion, similar in force and devarsetation to a bumcano eruption.

VITAL STATISTICS

Scientific name: *Stenchus gantori*
Family: Stenchosaur
Diet: Omnivorarse
Time: Crapaceous 135–65 mya
Stink rating: 🐾🐾🐾🐾🐾

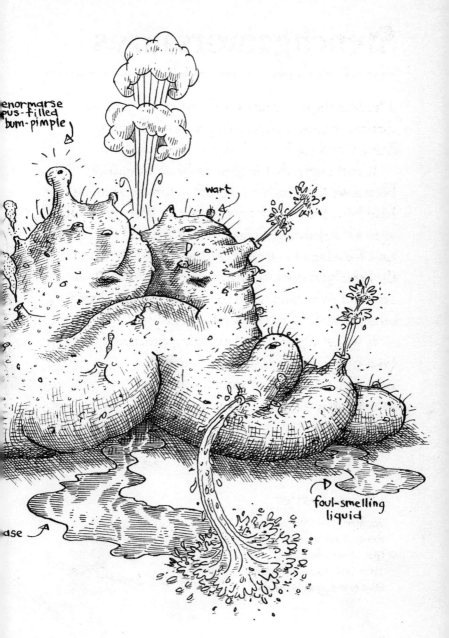

enormarse pus-filled bum-pimple

wart

foul-smelling liquid

ase

Tyrannosore-arse rex versus Tricerabutt

Besides eating and fighting, there was nothing bumosaurs liked better than eating and fighting. And if it was fighting and eating each other, then even better. This illarsestration is an artist's reconstruction of an actual fight based on fossilized remains of a Tyrannosore-arse rex and a Tricerabutt that died mid-fight when they were buried by a bogslide.

bumosaurus Bumadactyl Arseyopteryx Fartosaur
d mini bumosaurus Bumadactyl Arseyopteryx Fa
h-speed mini bumosaurus Bumadactyl Arse
erpantsosaurus High-speed mini bumosaurus
anobum Underpantsosaurus High-speed mini bum
Pteranobum Underpantsosaurus High-speed
hasaurus rex Pteranobum Underpantsosaurus
osaurus Flushasaurus rex Pteranobum Unde
yopteryx Fartosaurus Flushasaurus rex Pterai
adactyl Arseyopteryx Fartosaurus Flushasauru
osaurus Bumadactyl Arseyopteryx Fartosaurus F
bumosaurus Bumadactyl Arseyopteryx Fartosaur
d mini bumosaurus Bumadactyl Arseyopteryx Fa
h-speed mini bumosaurus Bumadactyl Arse
erpantsosaurus High-speed mini bumosaurus
anobum Underpantsosaurus High-speed mini bum
Pteranobum Underpantsosaurus High-speed
hasaurus rex Pteranobum Underpantsosaurus
osaurus Flushasaurus rex Pteranobum Unde
yopteryx Fartosaurus Flushasaurus rex Pterai
adactyl Arseyopteryx Fartosaurus Flushasauru
osaurus Bumadactyl Arseyopteryx Fartosaurus F
bumosaurus Bumadactyl Arseyopteryx Fartosaur
d mini bumosaurus Bumadactyl Arseyopteryx Fa
h-speed mini bumosaurus Bumadactyl Arse
erpantsosaurus High-speed mini bumosaurus
anobum Underpantsosaurus High-speed mini bum
Pteranobum Underpantsosaurus High-speed
hasaurus rex Pteranobum Underpantsosaurus
osaurus Flushasaurus rex Pteranobum Unde

Bumornithids

As competition on the land became ever keener
some of the bumosaurs began to take advantage
of the thrusting power of their gas emissions and
launched themselves into the air. Others
supplemented their gas power with large saggy
flaps of skin, which they used as primitive wings,
and gradually learned to master controlled flight.

BUMADACTYL

ARSEYOPTERYX

FARTOSAURUS

FLUSHASAURUS REX

PTERANOBUM

UNDERPANTSOSAURUS

HIGH-SPEED MINI BUMOSAURUS

Bumadactyl

The Bumadactyl was one of the first bums to take to the air. It had a vast wing-span of 50m, but its 'wings' were actually nothing more than large, loose, leathery flaps of bumcheek skin, and it gained most of its lift and speed from its abundant gas power.

Unfortunately, the Bumadactyl was at the mercy of its primitive, crudely formed bowels and would often go out of control, like a balloon that is blown up and then let go without its end being tied.

Clogging the skies during the late Triarssic period, Bumadactyls were largely responsible for the creation of the methane layer in the Earth's atmosphere.

VITAL STATISTICS

Scientific name: *Cheekum flaparsius*
Family: Flapposaurid
Diet: Carnivorarse
Time: Messozoic era 250–203 mya
Stink rating: 🐾 🐾 🐾 🐾 🐾

Bumadactyl flies out of control after gas explosion

Arseyopteryx

Arseyopteryx was the world's first true flying bum, as opposed to bums that just accidentally blasted themselves into the air as a result of unexpectedly violent emissions.

While Arseyopteryx certainly relied on the same basic thrusting power, it is thought that its ability to control its flight might have developed as a result of its having dry, flaky skin. The large, scale-like pieces of dry skin covering Arseyopteryx eventually became so pronounced that they formed the first primitive bum feathers, which in turn formed the first true wings.

As time went on, Arseyopteryx developed more flying skill and progressed from simple solo joy flights to being able to impress potential mates by putting on spectacular hot-air shows.

VITAL STATISTICS

Scientific name: *Plumae ridiculus*
Family: Arsornithine
Diet: Bum-seedivorarse
Time: Jurarssic 203–135 mya
Stink rating: 🖤🖤🖤🖤🖤

Fartosaurus

The Fartosaurus was a unique creature – a bumosaur that was formed from the floating gases of several other species of bumosaur. While the Fartosaurus lived a relatively peaceful life compared to other bumosaurs, it could, however, be extremely dangerous. It was capable of descending on its prey and smothering it whole in a silent but deadly manner.

Although it had no natural predators, the greatest threat to the Fartosaurus came from the natural elements. A Fartosaurus could easily be broken up and dissipated by strong winds, and due to its highly flammable nature would often burst into flames when struck by lightning.

VITAL STATISTICS

Scientific name: *Stinkius vaporarse*
Family: Gasornithid
Diet: Carnivorarse
Time: Jurarssic 203–135 mya
Stink rating: 💨💨💨💨💨

Flushasaurus rex

The Flushasaurus rex was not an ancient predecessor of the modern flush toilet as is often thought. In fact, despite sharing the same basic shape, they are not related at all.

The Flushasaurus rex had wings, legs and a barbed tail. Modern flush toilets have none of these. Another major difference is that the Flushasaurus rex did not dispose of waste like a modern toilet, but instead spent most of its time hurling great loads of dirty, smelly water out of its mouth. This was done in self-defence, as other bumosaurs were always trying to sit on it, which was probably due to the extreme shortage of modern flush toilets on Earth during the reign of the bumosaurs.

VITAL STATISTICS

Scientific name: *Vomitus projectilius*
Family: Freakasaurid
Diet: Carnivorarse
Time: Jurarssic 203–135 mya
Stink rating: 🐾🐾🐾🐾🐾

Pteranobum

The Pteranobum was one of the fiercest of the
flying bumosaurs. It spent most of its time flying
around and knocking other, smaller flying bumosaurs
out of the sky with the thick bony bum attached to
the end of its whip-like tail.

As the Pteranobum was herbivorarse, this
behaviour was not motivated so much by the need
for food as by the fact that it was just a bully that
liked picking on flying bumosaurs smaller than itself.

By the end of the Jurarssic period the other
bumosaurs had had enough of Pteranobum's bullying
and they would regularly gang up to take their revenge
on one by pushing its head into the mouth of a
Flushasaurus rex.

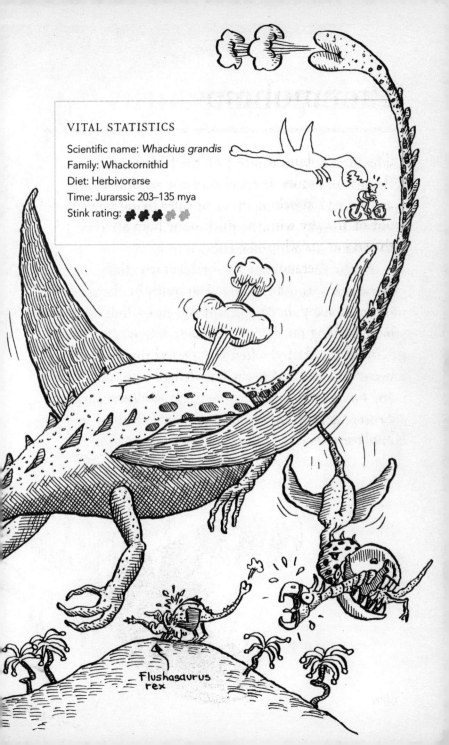

VITAL STATISTICS

Scientific name: *Whackius grandis*
Family: Whackornithid
Diet: Herbivorarse
Time: Jurarssic 203–135 mya
Stink rating: 🌸🌸🌸🌸🌸

Flushasaurus
rex

Underpantsosaurus

Underpantsosauruses mostly travelled in pairs, though they sometimes formed large groups known as multipacks. These multipacks sometimes contained so many Underpantsosauruses that they would form a cloud thick enough to block out the sun. Events such as these struck fear into the hearts of land-dwelling bumosaurs, which could imagine nothing worse than being trapped inside a big dirty stinky smelly pair of Underpantsosauruses.

Unlike most bumosaurs, the Underpantsosaurus did not die out completely, but rather bumvolved over many millions of years, becoming gradually smaller and more fashionable. During this process of bumolution the Underpantsosaurus lost its ability to fly and the more modern species were eventually domesticated by bum-men and kept in underpants drawers.

VITAL STATISTICS

Scientific name: *Jockus maximus*
Family: Knickersaurid
Diet: Carnivorarse
Time: Jurarssic 203–135 mya
Stink rating: ✿✿✿✿✿

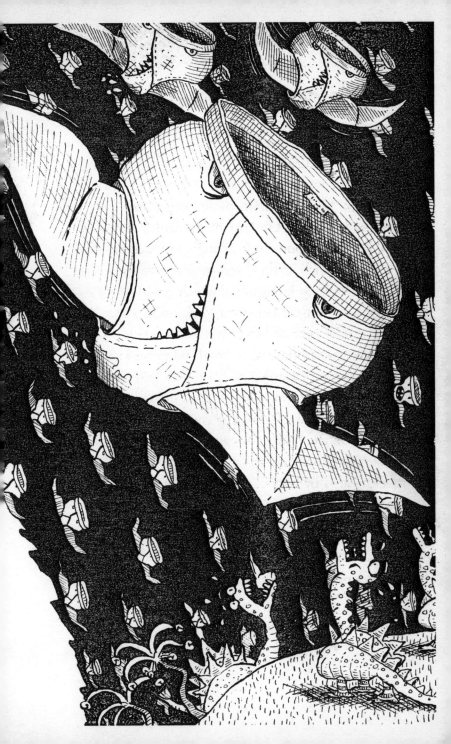

High-speed mini bumosaurus

The High-speed mini bumosaurus was so small and so fast that it could not be seen with the naked eye. In fact, this picture has only been made possible by the magic of high-speed illarsetration, a technique pooineered by the famarse bumosaur illarsetrator Jock MacDouglarse.

Bumosaurologists have speculated that the High-speed mini bumosaurus achieved its high speed thanks to a combination of explosive bursts of gas power and its aerobumnamically designed cheeks, which were hard and shiny and allowed it to cut through the air with minimum resistance.

Impossible to catch, the High-speed mini bumosaurus may well have lived forever, had windows not been invented.

VITAL STATISTICS

Scientific name: *Fastus hellus*
Family: Speedornithine
Diet: Bumteria-ivorarse
Time: Crapaceous 135–65 mya
Stink rating: 🐾🐾🐾🐾🐾

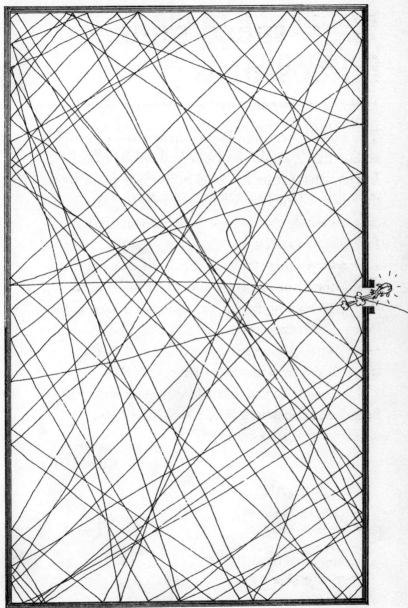

MAGNIFIED 1,000,000,000,000,000,000,000,000,000 TIMES

Exstinktion of the bumosaurs

There are many theories as to what caused the exstinktion of the bumosaurs, but the most likely explanation is the collision of a giant arseteroid with the Earth, around 65 million years ago. It probably looked something like this:

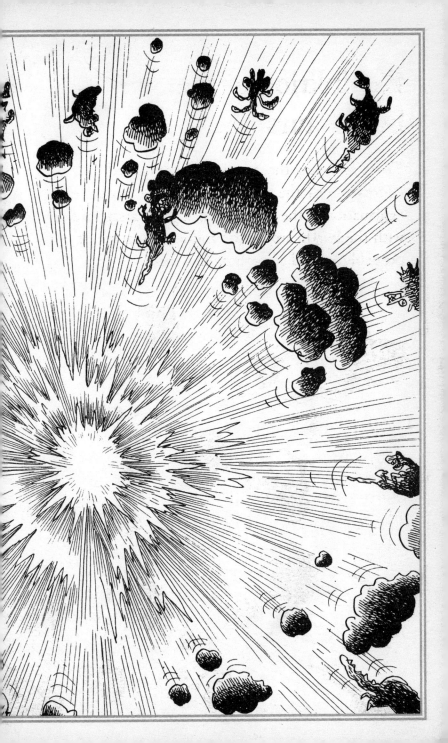

Bumanderthal   Loch Ness Bum-monster   Dis
minable Poo-man Bumanderthal Loch Ness Bum-m
Abuminable Poo-man Bumanderthal Loch Ness I
hed bum Abuminable Poo-man Bumanderthal Loc
e-toothed bum Abuminable Poo-man Bumanderth
head Sabre-toothed bum Abuminable Poo-man Bu
lly Butthead Sabre-toothed bum Abuminable Poo-r
it Woolly Butthead Sabre-toothed bum Abumir
ustagong Great Woolly Butthead Sabre-toothed bu
ster Disgustagong Great Woolly Butthead Sabre-to
-monster Disgustagong Great Woolly Butthead Sal
s Bum-monster Disgustagong Great Woolly Butthea
1 Ness Bum-monster Disgustagong Great Woo
anderthal Loch Ness Bum-monster Disgustagong C
    Bumanderthal   Loch Ness Bum-monster   Dis
minable Poo-man Bumanderthal Loch Ness Bum-m
Abuminable Poo-man Bumanderthal Loch Ness I
hed bum Abuminable Poo-man Bumanderthal Loc
e-toothed bum Abuminable Poo-man Bumanderth
head Sabre-toothed bum Abuminable Poo-man Bu
lly Butthead Sabre-toothed bum Abuminable Poo-r
it Woolly Butthead Sabre-toothed bum Abumir
ustagong Great Woolly Butthead Sabre-toothed bu
ster Disgustagong Great Woolly Butthead Sabre-to
1-monster Disgustagong Great Woolly Butthead Sal
s Bum-monster Disgustagong Great Woolly Butthea
1 Ness Bum-monster Disgustagong Great Woo
anderthal Loch Ness Bum-monster Disgustagong C
    Bumanderthal   Loch Ness Bum-monster   Dis
minable Poo-man Bumanderthal Loch Ness Bum-m

Bummals

While a few bumosaurs may have survived the
mass exstinktion at the end of the Crapaceous
period, the relative absence of bumosaurs created
opportunities for the bumolution of prehistoric
bummals, which led to the development of
Bumanderthals and their descendants, the earliest
bum-men (also known as humans).

LOCH NESS BUM-MONSTER

DISGUSTAGONG

GREAT WOOLLY BUTTHEAD

SABRE-TOOTHED BUM

ABUMINABLE POO-MAN

BUMANDERTHAL

Loch Ness bum-monster

The most famarse deep-water dwelling bummal is the Loch Ness bum-monster, which for hundreds of years has been reported to inhabit Loch Ness, an extraordinarily deep lake in Botland.

Evidence for the existence of this species is almost exclusively in the form of eyewitness accounts. People have reported seeing a bum or series of bums and an extremely long neck with a bum-shaped head rising from the water's surface.

The only piece of evidence that both experts and non-experts agree is one hundred per cent reliable is this picture of the Loch Ness bum-monster by world-famarse bumosaurologist, Jock MacDouglarse, who has seen and drawn the mysterious creature on at least three separate occasions.

VITAL STATISTICS

Scientific name: *Monsteri rectumius*
Family: Mysteriosaur
Diet: Unknown
Time: Perhaps Sewerian 435 mya to present
Stink rating: Unknown

Disgustagong

One of the most disgusting of all sea-going bummals, the Disgustagong had disgusting, stumpy little flippers and a disgusting, stupid-looking face and spent its time doing disgusting things like ▬▬▬▬▬▬▬ and ▬▬▬▬ and sometimes even ▬▬▬▬▬▬▬ ▬▬▬▬.

It could also often be heard making disgusting noises such as ▬▬▬▬▬▬▬!, ▬▬▬▬▬▬▬▬, ▬▬▬▬▬▬▬▬', and ▬▬▬▬▬▬▬▬'. But the most disgusting thing of all about the Disgustagong was when it vomited up bu▬▬▬▬▬▬ ▬▬▬▬▬▬▬▬ and ▬▬▬▬▬▬▬▬ ▬▬▬. ▬▬▬▬▬▬▬▬ all day long!

NOTE: The above passage has had certain lines blacked out because they are too disgusting for anyone to read.

VITAL STATISTICS

Scientific name: *Disgustaceous enormi*
Family: Bummal
Diet: ▬▬▬▬▬orarse
Time: Fartocene 65–1.75 mya
Stink rating: 🐾 🐾 🐾 🐾 🐾

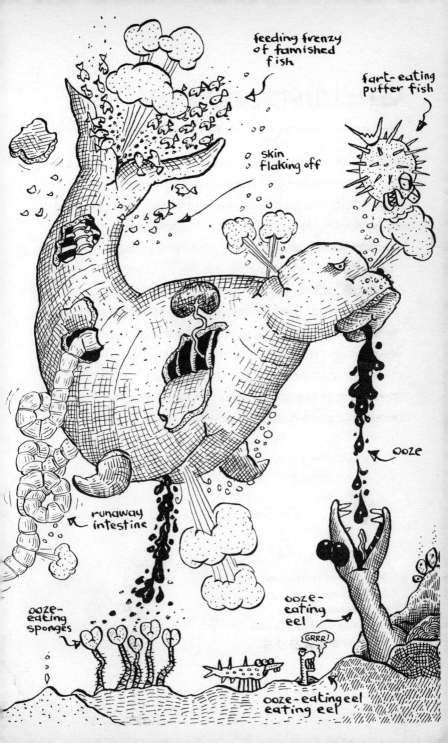

Great woolly butthead

Despite its vacant stare and less than flattering name, the Great woolly butthead was actually one of the most intelligent of the post-bumosaur Scentozoic era bummals, thanks to its two brains, located in its twin-cheeked forehead.

Admittedly, its thoughts, e.g. 'Why does everybody call me a butthead?' and 'What's for dinner?', could never be mistaken for those of a great philosopher. Nevertheless, this was thinking of an almost Einsteinian complexity compared to the 'thoughts' that had drifted occasionally through the tiny brown blobs that served as 'brains' for the average bumosaur, e.g. 'Stink', 'Kill', 'Eat', 'Wipe', 'Stink'.

VITAL STATISTICS

Scientific name: *Hirsutus cranium*
Family: Bummal
Diet: Herbivorarse
Time: Bumocene 1.75 mya – present
Stink rating:

Sabre-toothed bum

A highly aggressive bummal, the Sabre-toothed bum was one of the first post-bumosaur life forms to experiment with really big teeth.

These teeth were certainly useful for skewering both cheeks of an opponent at the same time, but ultimately proved to be more trouble than they were worth. When a Sabre-toothed bum sneezed, for example, the animal's head often snapped forward so violently that its fangs ended up piercing both its front feet and pinning them to the ground.

Mating also proved to be a hazardous affair. Even a simple kiss between a male and a female Sabre-toothed bum could result in the violent end of a courtship before it had even begun.

VITAL STATISTICS

Scientific name: *Posteria dentata*
Family: Bummal
Diet: Carnivorarse
Time: Bumocene 1.75 mya – present
Stink rating:

Abuminable Poo-man

Many bumolutionists now believe that the Abuminable Poo-man, long thought to be the stuff of legend, is actually the missing link between bummals and Bumanderthals.

In the Stinkalaya Mountains in Tibutt, where this creature is thought to live, locals refer to it as the Yucki, a Tibuttan word meaning 'big stinky poo-man'.

Reported sightings describe a large, hairy, poo-shaped ape that walks upright and attacks yaks, mountain climbers and mountain-climbing yaks.

Several expeditions have been organized to hunt down and capture a Yucki, but none have found more than bumprints, a few skidmarks and large brown blobs covered in coarse brown hair.

VITAL STATISTICS

Scientific name: *Homo turdus*
Family: Bummal
Diet: Carnivorarse
Time: Bumocene 1.75 mya – present
Stink rating: 💥💥💥💥💥

Bumanderthal

With their bottoms vastly reduced in size, modern
bum-men represent the triumph of brain over bum,
but with three bums – one behind, one on top and
one in front – Bumanderthal man was still more bum
than brain. Relatively primitive and unintelligent
creatures, they nevertheless tried their best to
communicate with each other, but their early
attempts at language were hampered by mid-sentence
eruptions of large quantities of gas, rude noises and
solid matter.

With three bums to look after, however,
Bumanderthals were obsessed with the quest for a
softer toilet paper, and many bumolutionists now
believe that this drive was largely responsible for the
subsequent growth of the brain and, in turn, the rise
of modern civilization.

VITAL STATISTICS

Scientific name: *Homo rectumus*
Family: Bummal
Diet: Omnivorarse
Time: Bumocene 1.75 mya – present
Stink rating: 🌸🌸🌸🌸🌸

Famarse bumosaurologists

Everything we know about bumosaurs and the prehistoric bum world is the result of the hard work and dedication of the scientists known as bumosaurologists. Here are the brief biographies of just a few of these unsung heroes.

Mary and Louis Gasleaky
A husband-and-wife team whose fossil finds proved that bumosaurs were much smellier than had previously been thought.

Eric Von Dunnycan
Author of *Chariots of the Bums*, a book in which he claims that Great white bumosauruses were actually bums from another planet.

Sir Roger Francis Rectum
Author of *The Origins of the Univarse* in which The Theory of Bumolution was first explained.

Jock MacDouglarse
Inventor of high-speed illarsetration, which made possible the first-ever glimpse of the High-speed mini bumosaurus. He is also the only person to have illarsestrated the elusive Loch Ness bum-monster.

Charles Bumwin
Discovered one of the most famous fossil finds in the history of bumosaurology: prehistoric skidmarks preserved on the surface of an ancient bumcano bog-flow.

small fart hatch →

Index

Also by
ANDY GRIFFITHS
the bumolutionary **BUM** trilogy

THE DAY MY BUM WENT PSYCHO

ZOMBIE BUMS FROM URANUS

BUMAGEDDON ...THE FINAL PONGFLICT

in which **Zack**, **the hero**, travels back in time to when **Bumosaurs ruled the world.**

CHAPTER 28

TRICERABUTT

The bum-fighters fought their way through the shaded semi-tropical undergrowth. Zack wiped his sweating brow and marvelled at the difference that 585 million years can make. The Earth had come alive. There were bumnut-tree forests in place of grey sludge. Giant mutant blowflies droned around their heads. Enormous red stinkants lumbered in single file across the forest floor. And, of course, terrifying bumosaurs ruled the planet.

As they hacked against thick vines and even thicker spider webs, the bum-fighters could hear Robobum preparing to do battle with the tyrannosore-arses.

'I must warn you,' said Robobum, 'I have fully riveted reinforced steel cheeks. Turbo-assisted jet repulsion units . . .'

There was a loud tyrannosore-arse howl.

A sickening metallic crunch.

And then . . . silence.

Zack glanced back at Ned.

Ned looked at Zack.

'Nuclear wart-head equipped,' said a voice. 'Matter transport assisted entry and exit. Inside and outside voice options. Onboard tea- and coffee-making . . .'

The bum-fighters grinned with relief. But not for long.

There was another howl.

Followed by another crunch.

Silence.

And then . . .

'. . . and I am self-wiping!'

A third crunch.

And a fourth.

And a fifth.

Ned put his hands over his ears. 'Robobum!' he cried. 'My Robobum!'

'Come on, Ned,' said Eleanor, putting her arm around his shoulders. 'We have to look after ourselves now. It's what Robobum would want.'

Zack, who was leading, pushed his way into a rectangular clearing that was about the size of a football pitch.

'Hey!' said his bum, trying to brighten the mood. 'Anyone for football?'

'We don't have a ball,' said Ned.

'We could use Zack's bum,' said Eleanor.

'Not funny!' said Zack's bum.

They were halfway across the clearing when Zack screamed.

'Shut up!' said Eleanor. 'Do you want the tyrannosore-arses to hear us?'

'No,' said Zack. 'But . . .'

'But what?' said Eleanor.

Zack was speechless.

He could only point.

Charging towards them was a huge armoured bum with three cheeks. Each cheek had a large wart in its centre.

And each wart was sharpened to a deadly point.

'Oh no,' said Ned, looking from his guidebook to the bumosaur and then back to the book. 'A tricerabutt!'

'We can see that!' said Zack's bum. 'How do you stop it?'

'You can't,' said Ned, consulting his book. 'It says here that nothing can stop a charging tricerabutt.'

They all stared helplessly at the triple-cheeked beast as it lumbered towards them, picking up speed as it came.

Zack gulped.

In the space of a single morning they'd been giant-brown-blobbified, travelled millions of years into the past, been involved in a wild bum chase, travelled millions of years into the future and been attacked by not one, but *two* tyrannosore-arses. They needed a tricerabutt attack like they needed a hole in the head . . . or *three* holes, as was a very real possibility in this situation.

'Gee,' said Zack. 'The Cretaceous is a really fun place. We should come here more often.'

'We'll be lucky to get out alive,' said Eleanor.

The tricerabutt snorted as it ran.

The stink made Zack feel faint.

The bum-fighters were in trouble.

Big trouble.

Bad trouble.

Triple trouble.

They didn't have time to run back to where they'd come from. The jungle was too dense. And running forward was out of the question.

Then Zack had an idea.

'Stand back, everyone,' he said.

'What are you going to do?' said Zack's bum, backing away with Ned and Eleanor.

Zack pulled what was left of his bum-fighter's certificate out of his bum-fighting belt and, using the two top corners, held it out to his side, matador-style.

'Be careful, Zack!' said his bum.

' "Careful" is my middle name,' said Zack.

'No, it's not,' said his bum. 'It's Henry!'

'Shut up!' said Zack.

Zack Henry Freeman took a deep breath and focused. 'You want a piece of me?' he said to the charging tricerabutt. 'Come and get it!'

has begun!

Are you brave enough to fight the bum invaders?
Log on to www.bumageddon.com, select your weapon
of choice and brown-blobbify the evil bum invaders.
You could be crowned the world's best bum-fighter!

www. **BUMAGEDDON** .com

And not forgetting the *JUST* hilarious books
by Andy Griffiths and Terry Denton:

*Just Annoying! Just Crazy! Just Disgusting!
Just Kidding! Just Stupid!*

Are they just the books for you?
Take the test to find out!

YES	NO	
☐	☐	Do you ever pretend that you are dead to get out of going to school?
☐	☐	Do you ask 'Are we there yet?' over and over on long car trips?
☐	☐	Do you automatically turn around when somebody calls, 'Hey, Stupid!'?
☐	☐	Do you ever look in the mirror and see a maniac staring back at you?
☐	☐	Do you think Brussels sprouts are a delicious mouth-watering treat?

SCORE: **One point for each 'yes' answer**

3–5 You are utterly disgusting, a joking genius beyond compare and a maniac capable of extremely irritating and bonkers behaviour. Well done! You will love these books.

1–2 You are fairly disgusting, fairly annoying, a bit of a joker, a little on the stupid side, not completely crazy, but not far off either. You will still love these books.

0 You just don't appreciate how much fun being extremely annoying, crazy, disgusting, stupid and a complete kidder can be. Nonetheless, you will love these books.

A selected list of titles available from
Macmillan Children's Books

The prices shown below are correct at the time of going to press. However, Macmillan Publishers resewes the right to show new retail prices on covers, which may differ from those previously advertised.

Andy Griffiths

Just Annoying!	978-0-330-39729-2	£4.99
Just Crazy!	978-0-330-39729-8	£4.99
Just Disgusting!	978-0-330-41592-7	£4.99
Just Kidding!	978-0-330-39728-5	£4.99
Just Stupid!	978-0-330-39726-1	£4.99
The Day My Bum Went Psycho	978-0-330-40089-3	£4.99
Zombie Bums from Uranus	978-0-330-43680-9	£4.99
Bumageddon . . . The Final Pongflict	978-0-330-43370-9	£4.99

Frank Cottrell Boyce

Framed	978-0-330-43425-6	£5.99
Millions	978-0-330-43331-0	£5.99

All Pan Macmillan titles can be ordered from our website, www.panmacmillan.com, or from your local bookshop and are also available by post from:

Bookpost, PO Box 29, Douglas, Isle of Man IM99 IBQ
Credit cards accepted. For details:
Telephone: 01624 677237
Fax: 01 624 670923
Email: bookshop@enterprise.net
www.bookpost.co.uk

Free postage and packing in the United Kingdom